A JOURNAL OF CONTEMPORARY WRITING

IRISH PAGES

DUILLÍ ÉIREANN

IRISH PAGES is a biannual journal (Spring/Summer, Autumn/Winter), edited in Belfast and publishing, in equal measure, writing from Ireland and overseas. It appears at the end of each six-month period.

Its policy is to publish poetry, short fiction, essays, creative non-fiction, memoir, essay reviews, nature-writing, translated work, literary journalism, and other autobiographical, historical, religious and scientific writing of literary distinction. There are no standard reviews or narrowly academic articles. Irish language and Ulster Scots writing are published in the original, with English translations or glosses.

IRISH PAGES is a non-partisan, non-sectarian, culturally ecumenical, and wholly independent journal. It endorses no political outlook or cultural tradition, and has no editorial position on the constitutional question. Its title refers to the island of Ireland in a purely apolitical and geographic sense, in the same manner of The Church of Ireland or the Irish Sea.

The sole criteria for inclusion in the journal are the distinction of the writing and the integrity of the individual voice. Equal editorial attention will be given to established, emergent and new writers.

The views expressed in IRISH PAGES are not necessarily those of the Editors. The magazine has no editorial or financial connection to the Linen Hall Library or its Directors.

Submissions are welcome but must be accompanied by return postage or an international reply coupon. No self-addressed envelope is required. Reporting time is six months. If work is accepted, a copy on disk may be requested.

Your subscription is essential to the independence and survival of the journal. Subscription rates are £16/€26/$34 for one year, or £24/€39/$46 for two years. For postage outside Ireland and Britain, add £4/€6/$8 per year for Europe, or £6/€9/$12 per year for the rest of the world. Visit our website at www.irishpages.org for a subscription form. Credit cards are welcome.

IRISH PAGES
The Linen Hall Library
17 Donegall Square North
Belfast BT1 5GB

IRISH PAGES is designed by Tonic and set in 12/14 Monotype Perpetua.
It is printed in Belfast by Nicholson & Bass.

This issue has been generously asssisted by Foras na Gaeilge and the Arts Councils of Northern and Southern Ireland.

ISBN 978-0-9544257-8-4

Foras na Gaeilge

arts council of Northern Ireland

the arts council an chomhairle ealaíon

IRISH PAGES

CHRIS AGEE, *Editor*

CATHAL Ó SEARCAIGH, *Irish Language Editor*

SEÁN MAC AINDREASA, *Managing Editor*

EDITED IN BELFAST
VOLUME 4, NUMBER 2

IRISH PAGES
DUILLÍ ÉIREANN

VOLUME 4, NUMBER 2

CONTENTS

Hong Kong, 1974

by John Minihan

THE KINGDOM OF MANANNÁN

Tim Robinson

Sea-cousins.

Once when the tide was far out and the sleek black mud bottom of Roundstone harbour was revealed, two little girls poking around down there hailed me as I passed by on the quayside and told me to come and see what they had found. So I went down by the slip and trod warily out to them. What they had was a slimy brown clump of something stringy, which they were trying to untangle. A bootlace worm, I pronounced, and suggested that when they had finished looking at it they should put it back where they found it. "Oh I know!" said the elder of them, casting her eyes up to heaven with heavy sarcasm; "It has just as much right to life as I do ..." "Good girls", said I doubtfully, and left them to it.

Back among my books I looked up the bootlace worm. *Linneus longissimus* is its name, and it is often five yards long, while specimens of thirty or more yards have been unravelled, though it tends to tie itself in knots when handled and breaks very easily. It is usually about a tenth of an inch across, but can contract and thicken itself or stretch itself out thinner. It is an unsegmented worm or nemertine, and it lives on small segmented or bristle worms. It exudes slime and lives in a coiled mass under stones, but can progress smoothly by means of ripples passing along its body from tail to head. It has ten to twenty obscure little eyes.

I saw the elder girl again later on. "Did you put that worm back?" I asked. "No!" she screamed fiercely, "We dropped rocks on the yucky thing!"

If some marine life-forms are repellent in their strangeness, others appal by a beauty that chills, being so evidently not addressed to us. When I rang the ecologist Cilian Roden, to ask him something about the bootlace worm, he told me there was an image on the NASA website I should look at, a satellite photograph of an algal bloom in the Atlantic off Slyne Head. I called it up on my screen: a milky-blue curdling five hundred miles long, curled and combed by sea-currents, consisting of quadrillions of coccolithophores. I knew something of the coccolithophore, a single-celled planktonic plant. Once when I called in to the Marine Research Centre of the University in Galway to ask about the foraminifera found in Dog's Bay, which I was writing about at the time, the researchers there agreed that "forams" were mightily abundant and quaintly shaped entities – but had I ever seen the coccolithophores? – and they got out a coffee-table-format book of electron micrographs to show me. These less-than-dust-sized organisms – of which half a million could fit on the head of a pin – have spherical shells made up of plates of calcium carbonate; some species grow these plates or "coccoliths" in large numbers and shed them constantly, while others produce just the twenty or so needed to cover themselves, which are released when the plant dies. It is the lime-white clouds of coccoliths swept together in a gyre of the ocean and reflecting the sun's rays as they drift down to the seabed that turn vast stretches of water into milk now and again.

Leafing through the hundreds of illustrations in this book of different species of these plants and the distinctive coccoliths each species produces, I was moved as never before, both frightened and overjoyed, by nature's fecundity of form. The coccolith in general has the shape of a tube, shorter than it is wide, with a broad flange around either end, like a hat with two brims, the outer end of the tube being open and the inner end closed by a grill of radial elements. The details are endlessly varied, each specimen, when enlarged a few hundred thousand times, looking like a caprice of the ceramicist's art. And yet it seems that these extraordinary confections come into being quite automatically. A vast deal of research has gone into studying this process, which takes place within the plant cell and uses the lime dissolved in seawater: a ring of calcium carbonate crystals is laid down, each of which then grows at different rates in very specific directions, to build up the two-flanged tube with all its never-to-be-seen detailing. When complete the coccolith is extruded onto the surface of the cell, where by random jostling it fits itself in among the others, all interlocked by means of their flanges. Presumably the initial ring of crystals is formed on a template of some complicated protein, which in its turn has been precisely engineered by the genetic machinery, directed by DNA, of the coccolithophore species – but all this fantastic collaboration of crystallographic and biochemical processes remains to be figured out. Nor is it known what the coccoliths are for! Perhaps the whole structure, the "coccosphere", enclosing the cell retains some water between the two layers of flanges, surrounding the plant with an environment the chemistry of which it can control; perhaps the plates protect the plant against viruses or make it less attractive to plankton-eaters; perhaps they adjust the buoyancy of the plant and keep it within some range of depths; perhaps like lenses they deflect sunlight into the cell to further photosynthesis. Nobody knows; the answer probably involves some or all of these possibilities, and others, evolution by natural selection being so efficient an exploiter of what is to hand.

And in the end the coccolithophore, however well adjusted it is to its environment, dies, and its armature breaks up and falls like a slow snow into the ocean ooze, which over millions of years is compressed into rock. All that ingenious geometry is compounded into bulk material. The Downs of southern England, the White Cliffs of Dover, are built of coccoliths.

*

Now, of all Connemara's shores by which one might meditate on the alterity of sea-life, one in particular proposes itself, by its name, as the most suitable: Mannin Bay, a mile or so north of Ballyconneely. Manannán mac Lir whose patronymic, meaning "son of the sea", shows him to be a sea god, was (or is) the Celtic Poseidon. Like the Greek god he is a shape-shifter, an ungraspable master of disguise. He makes several appearances in the lore of the Fianna, Fionn Mac Cumhal's warrior band; sometimes he is helpful, sometimes a tease, and sometimes both. For instance when the Fianna are challenged to a race by a stranger called Caol and Fionn is looking for a champion to represent them, he meets "Bodach an Chóta Lachtna", the grey-cloaked lout, in the forest, who offers to take up the challenge. The course set is from Howth Head to Sliabh Luachra in Kerry, and back again. Caol sets off at a great pace, but the grey-cloaked lout overtakes him despite stopping for huge meals. When Caol tells him that he has left tatters of his cloak on a thornbush the lout thanks him and goes back to collect them and sew them on again, before passing out Caol with the speed of the wind and winning the race. When the wind and the sun light up the lout's face Fionn recognizes him as Manannán mac Lir.

In another complicated and rambling story the god plays the role of the Ceithearnach Caolriabhaigh, the narrow-striped kern or soldier, a joker and conjuror in striped clothing, who among other tricks casts a silken thread up into the air so that it is made fast to a cloud, takes a hare out of his bag and sends it running up the thread, takes a dog out of the bag and sends it in pursuit of the hare, produces a little serving-boy and sends him after hare and dog, and finally a beautiful girl to follow after the rest. When a commotion breaks out in the cloud he hauls in the thread. On finding that the dog is chewing the bones of the hare and the lad has "gone between the two legs of the lady" he strikes the lad's head off and puts it on again back to front, but then relents and twists it around to the right position.

> And with that the man of tricks vanished, and no one saw where was he gone. That is the way Manannan used to be going round Ireland, doing tricks and wonders. And no one could keep him in any place, and if he was put on a gallows itself, he would be found safe in the house after, and some other man on the gallows in his place. But he did no harm, and those that would be put to death by him, he would bring them to life again with a herb out of his bag.

But it is on the sea that the god appears in his true majesty. The story of Saint Scaithín walking across a flowery plain and meeting Saint Barre sailing in a boat, which I told in connection with Inishbofin, is a brief Christianized echo of a meeting with Manannán described in an eighth-century wonder-tale, *The Voyage of Bran*. Wandering near his royal house one day Bran hears sweet music, and falls asleep to it. When he awakes he sees a silver branch bearing white blossoms, and takes it home with him. There a woman in strange raiment appears and sings fifty quatrains, explaining that the silver branch is from the apple tree of Emhain, an incomparably beautiful island "without grief, without death, without sickness". Then she disappears, taking the silver branch with her. The next day Bran, with three companies of nine of his followers, puts to sea. After rowing for two days and two nights they see a man in a chariot coming towards them over the sea – Manannán mac Lir, who sings them thirty quatrains, beginning:

> Caíne amra laisin mBran
> ina churchán tar muir nglan;
> os mé, am charput do chéin,
> is magh sccothach ima-réidh.

Scholars have rendered the beautiful obscurities of Manannán's song in irreconcilable ways; I condense their efforts freely, in the wake of the concise antitheses of the original:

> Bran delights in sailing his currach on the pure sea,
> which for me is a flowery plain my chariot crosses from afar.
> Bran sees numberless breaking waves, where I see perfect red blossoms.
> Sea horses glisten in summer as far as Bran can cast his eye.
> In the kingdom of Mannnán rivers flow with honey.
> You see speckled salmon leaping from the sea's white womb;
> they are calves and particoloured lambs peacefully at play.
> Men and gentle women at wine under a bush play a delightful blameless game.
> From the beginning of things we are ageless,
> facing no loss of freshness, exempt from original sin.

Manannán goes on to predict that he himself will lie with a queen and father a son, Mongan (who is a historical figure; he was a prince of Dál nAraid in Ulster and died in 624 AD, according to the Annals). Bran and his crew then sail on to blissful adventures in the Land of Women, where there is a bed and a bed-companion for each of his thrice-nine followers. After what seems like a year but must have been centuries they return to within shouting distance of Ireland; one of them leaps ashore and immediately crumbles into ashes. Bran tells the people there his name, and they say they don't know him but that *The Voyage of Bran* is among their ancient stories. Bran tells them his adventures, and leaves an account of them in ogham. He then sails off again, "and from that hour his wanderings are not known".

When gods became obsolete and reinvented themselves as heroes Manannán became a sea-trader from the Isle of Man, which was anciently called Mana; according to a ninth-century glossary "he was the greatest navigator of this western part of the world, and used to presage good or bad weather from his observation of the heavens, and from the changes of the moon". Manannán has especially close connections with Connemara. The Conmaicne sept of Leinster, who later moved into Connacht, knew him under the name of Oirbsiu and regarded him as their ancestor. Presumably it was the branch of the sept known as the Conmaicne Mara, the Conmaicne of the sea, from whom Connemara is named, who brought his cult to the lands west of Galway. Their traditions held that he was killed in a battle at Moycullen, was buried standing up, and that the great lake, Loch nOirbsen, now corruptly known as Lough Corrib, burst forth from his grave. This flood is not the only example of the sea-god's mastery of geography; like Poseidon again he is an earth-shaker. There is a little island called Oileán Mana off Cill Chiaráin in south Connemara that according to local folklore was called into existence by Manannán to save his daughter when her boat was caught in a storm there. Mannin Bay too is named from him, says Hardiman, the Galway historian, writing in the 1840s, but exactly why this should be so is, I believe, unknown.

*

Mannin Bay, then, would seem to be a privileged site for a consideration of the strangeness of that zone disputed twice a day between the strange but familiar land of Connemara and the strange and unfamiliar realm of Manannán. Having talked with Cilian of such extravagant entities as the numberless coccolithophores and the immeasurable worm, I suggested we go down to the sea at Mannin to defamiliarize ourselves with some of the more familiar creatures in its margins. We left it till late in the summer, when the rockpools should be hopping with sun-fuelled life, and chose a day of spring tides and the hour of deepest ebb. I persuaded some other friends and mentors along too: Cilian's partner Sabine Springer, marine biologist and illustrator of seashore life, the poet Moya Cannon, and Máirtín O'Malley, whose dealings with the sea are so multifarious we call him the Ambassador of the Ocean. Mannin is the widest of Connemara's west-facing bays; about three miles of water separate Errislannan, its northern shore, from Errismore or Iorras Mór, the big peninsula, to the south. The Coral Strand is the finest of the beaches that line the head of the bay, with the coast road passing immediately inland of them. When we stood out of our cars in the carpark above the sea wall there and stretched ourselves it was around midday (spring high waters being affairs of dawn and dusk in these parts, and low waters in between them). The wind was light and the waves, *capaill Mhanannán*, Manannán's horses, as Irish folklore knows them, were pasturing peaceably far out in the bay. A long hazy sector of horizon stretched between the rockbound point of Errislannan and the little hill of

Knock three miles away to the west where the Iorras Mór coastline turns southwards and runs out to the last lonely land's-end of Connemara, Slyne Head. Beyond that lay, we knew, the coccolithic bloom seen from space as a milky way, and the Porcupine Bank, teeming with fish, and the recently discovered sea mounts about which Michael Viney has written so eloquently, submarine pyramids and towers of coral hosting fantastic worlds of creatures barely known to science. However, our appointment was not with those unreachable wonders, but the little everyday, every-tide, doorkeepers of the near waters, the ebb and flow. There was a note of celebration in the sea breeze, perhaps because Moya, gentle creature of gold dust and heather pollen, had sufficiently recovered from illness to be with us, perhaps because beaches bring us back to a primal time of life. We tumbled onto the sands like the children of her poem "Shells":

> We used to hunker on the Silver Strand,
> sifting the shells after a storm, hunting for cowries.
>
> The pink, furled nuggets were stored in jam jars,
> hoarded in jacket pockets, on windowsills,
> with pelicans' feet,
> razor shells,
> scallop shells,
> turret shells
> and the rare, white wentletrap.
>
> Ignorant of how Venus had sailed ashore,
> we were already intrigued
> by all the felt asymmetries of the small sea-beasts' growth,
> all the dizzy architecture
> of the first flesh.

The Coral Strand too is silvery, glimmery, moon-pale, and it crunches underfoot pleasantly; pick up a handful of its beach and you see it is composed of tiny twiglike bits of something like unglazed pottery, white, cream-coloured, pale green or faintly violet-flushed. This is not strictly coral, which is an animal product, but fragments broken off a coraline alga, a seaweed that draws on the calcium carbonate dissolved in seawater to stiffen its fronds with a limey deposit. Farther down the beach one finds bigger branchy pieces like stag's horns and, near the low tide mark, roundish bushes of it an inch or two across that have been floated ashore attached to the holdfasts of the big kelp seaweeds thrown up by storms. There are a few such coral-beaches in Connemara, of which this and An Trá Choiréalach near An Cheathrú Rua are the finest. The offshore, deep-water thickets of living maerl, as the several sorts of coralline seaweed are known collectively, provide nooks and crannies for an abundance of lurking, gliding, tube-building, tunnel-boring and sedentary sea-dwellers – I have seen an impressive list of the species recorded from Mannin Bay – and a vast fractal surface area for encrusting algae to colonize, and for specialized prostrate seaweeds to peg themselves onto, helping to storm-proof the maerl beds on which they depend for security.

Down at the water's rippling fringes we gathered around a boulder draped in dripping seaweed on which brightly coloured winkles were slowly cruising to and fro licking up the surface film of bacteria, and listened to Cilian proclaiming the priority and superior multiformity of marine life over terrestrial life. The genetic froth of evolution investing every possible habitat the sea offered eventually threw a splash of foam onto the shore, a few species, a few Venuses, from which all land-dwellers and their loves are derived. Thus only four phyla or major categories of many-celled animal species are represented on land, while there are about thirty-five phyla in the sea. Radial symmetry is unknown in terrestrial life-forms, but there were several exemplars of it for Cilian to point out, stuck to the boulder at hand: beadlet anemones, plump blood-red sacks with one central aperture above, encircled by two hundred or so short tentacles and necklaced with twenty-four blue spots – the beadlets, only visible when the creature is under water and open, for when the tide withdraws it swallows its tentacles and purses itself up, perfectly justifying its Irish name, *bundún leice*, arsehole of the rock.

In the water around the foot of the boulder Sabine pointed out a beautiful snakelocks anemone, grey-green with tinges of many other colours; she bade me put my finger to it and feel the soft clinging of its long wavy tentacles, to let it investigate us as we were investigating it. We looked at limpets clamped to rocks; to survive the hours of exposure they have to keep water within their shells, and therefore they always return to the same spot on their rock after roving around and grazing, and fit themselves onto it exactly. Where the rock is soft, as in the limestone Aran Islands, it is the stone that is worn into a perfect fit for the shell, but here on the hard metamorphic rocks of Connemara it is the shell that has to adapt itself to the stone. Then Máirtín wrestled over a big hunk of rock in a pool and exposed various disparate sea-beings. Soon I had, lying on my hand for Moya to photograph their "dizzy architecture", four sea-beasts that differed as much from each other as they did from me: a cushion starfish, like a plump little pentagonal badge; the well-named sea gherkin, finger-long, whitish, with ten feathery tentacles at one end; a purple heart-urchin, heart-shaped indeed and covered in pale spines; and a reddish periwinkle Cilian said was unusual, for what reason I have forgotten. Meanwhile Sabine, who has micro-sharp eyes as her delicate drawings of sea-creatures witness, roved among the rockpools and brought back curiosities to show me, so fine as to be transparent: a bryozoan or sea-mat, like a patch of velvety net appliquéd onto a seaweed-frond, each compartment of the net containing a tentacular Charybdis too small to see without a lens; and a hydroid, which looked like a tiny plant rooted on a bit of seaweed, but was actually a "ramified animal" with numerous anemone-like polyps on slender branches. This latter sea-wonder practises "alternation of generations", Sabine told me; the hydroid produces buds that become detached and float off like jellyfish, and breed sexually, discharging their ova and sperm into the water, the offspring settling to the bottom and growing into the next generation of attached hydroids like their grandparents.

Enough! There is no end to the weirdness of Manannán's subjects. The incoming tide was beginning to lift the seaweed tresses, billions of hungry little arms were reaching out into the flux of rotting seaweed-dust and plankton. We returned our finds to their niches, pocketed our lenses and Guides to the Sea Shore, and turned inland. But before we left the intertidal zone we had to stop and consider the barnacle, how it grows. Thousands of them – thirty thousand or more per square yard, say the reference books – armour the rocks with their sharp, hard, studs. Barnacles, though fixed in place like rivets, and hermaphrodite, still manage to interbreed, reaching their neighbours by means of penises up to an inch and a half long. The sperm and the ova come together within the little tent of limy plates that immures each individual, and the result, four months later, is a host of microscopic larvae that bear no obvious resemblance to their parents, clearly being crustaceans rather than molluscs, as barnacles were long assumed to be. They swim off, feed, grow, moult a few times, and eventually fix themselves to a rock by means of a cement exuded by glands on the head. Then they create their protective plates of calcium carbonate, which they extract from seawater as do so many other marine life-forms. Inside this drought- and predator-defying castle, with its roofplates that can be opened like the dome of an observatory, the animal totally rearranges its bodily parts so that its ten legs become feathery feelers it can wave out from its roof-aperture to trawl through the drift of sea-dust for edible particles.

Barnacle larvae are apparently a main constituent of the plankton pullulating in rockpools in summer, along with swarms of the sperm, eggs and young of hundreds of other species. Each sperm and ovum is as intensely alive, as unique, as the individual to which they may, against millionfold odds, give rise if they happen to pair up. Each bears a half-burden of genetic specification from parental to filial generation; it makes as much sense to say that the generations of individuals exist to produce the intermediate generations of "dividuals" as the other way round. We too swim in such a continuous stream of life; ethicists and legalists have to inscribe divisions in it as best they may, but this is for our own debatable purposes; there is no "fact of the matter" written in the stars to guide us. And it is equally important for us to feel this continuity, feel how it reaches back generation by generation to the rock pools, to the primeval slimes of self-replicating chemicals and perhaps to some extraterrestrial spawn of earth-life, blowing in the solar wind.

Finally, how is it that such minute creatures can be so complex, that such almost impalpable parcels can hold so much – anatomies, senses, instincts – and in their short lives can go through such profound reorganizations of themselves? The answer, I think, is that seen in the right perspective these creatures are huge. This perspective is not that of atomic physics, though that already makes the barnacle larva elephantine, an atom being so very much smaller than it, say a million times smaller, while an atomic particle such as a proton, millions of times smaller than an atom, has its own elaborate and dynamic interior structure. No, there is a deeper perspective that opens up from an idea due to the quantum theorist Max Planck. He showed that there is something like a least length, below which the concept of a length is meaningless; this "Planck length" is a naturally arising unit with which to measure greater lengths – and it is small beyond all imagining, being a million million billion times smaller than a proton. In terms of this unit the size of one of the rockpool's motes of life would contain so many zeros that the difference between that and our own size could easily be missed. So the simplest larva and even the single-celled coccolithophore has room for a universe of complexities. And since there is also a matching Planck time (it is that taken by a photon of light to travel the Planck length), the lifespan of the barnacle as measured in those units is of scarcely conceivable length and allows time for almost endless reactions and reconstructions.

So, having recognized some of these strange little creatures – recognized them from their descriptions and photographs in our reference books, and recognized them in their strangeness as our sea-cousins – we adapted our eyes once more to a human perspective, and turned for home. As Sabine remarked, we didn't have to make a long journey to see such marvels; we were only a hundred yards from our cars. And the beach watched as we, perhaps the strangest of all creatures, with glacial slowness lifted our gigantic heads out of the seaweed, blinked our meagre allowance of eyes, balanced ourselves on towering appendages, locomoted by a succession of arrested fallings forward, communicated by waves of agitation of air molecules, pairwise brought the lateral surfaces of our heads into centuries-long brief contacts (a behaviour the purpose of which is unknown), bent our spinal cords to coil ourselves into our waiting coccospheres, and, rolling on wheels, a device unknown among the people of Manannán, departed – strange to each other, strange to ourselves, fit denizens for this strangest of all impossible universes.

The above extract is a chapter from the forthcoming third volume of Tim Robinson's trilogy on Connemara.

Tim Robinson worked as a visual artist in Vienna and London before moving to the Aran Islands where he lived from 1972 to 1984. He now lives in Roundstone, Co Galway. One of Ireland's leading prose writers, he has published six volumes of non-fiction, including the two-volume Stones of Aran *(Lilliput Press, 1987, 1995),* Setting Foot on the Shores of Connemara *(Lilliput Press, 1996) and* My Time in Space *(Lilliput Press, 2001), as well as maps of Connemara, the Aran Islands and the Burren. He is also the author of a work of accumulated fictions,* Tales and Imaginings *(Lilliput Press, 2002). His most recent volumes of non-fiction are* Connemara: Listening to the Wind *(Penguin Ireland, 2006), and* Connemara: The Last Pool of Darkness *(Penguin Ireland, 2008).*

EDGE OF THE TIDE

Michael Viney

Infinite chance, infinite time.

The length of Ireland's coastline must now, I suppose, be nearing some kind of exactitude, as Earth is scanned obsessively by robots in the sky. But everything depends on where you pace it, and at what moment. Tide lifts and falls; foam reaches up to lick one's boots or curl around a rock. For the beachcomber, the boundary of land and ocean is more a state of mind than any line drawn in the sand. I have been walking the tideline, on and off, for much of my life, each visit a reminder that Earth is very big and I am, in its cosmos, very small.

The town where I was young – Brighton, on the English Channel – had a shingle beach, seasonally overlaid with thousands of striped towels and prostrate bodies. But in winter, with the stones washed clean and gleaming, it was possible to step back into the Victorian passion for pebble-collecting. A small, old-fashioned shop off the seafront dazzled me with semi-precious lapidary art: carved and polished onyx, jasper, agate, chalcedony, citrine, carnelian, amethyst – such mystical, ravishing names, and their glowing beauty, implicitly, the gift of the sea. Crunching along beside the waves, I made my choice from the millions of potential gems, and, emptying them out at home, tried to lick them back to life. Nothing in my education matched our pebble beaches to the story of the Earth, but in the crashing of breakers, the hiss of rolling stones, I did make some connection with the planetary world.

Ireland, too, has pebble strands, from the great storm-beaches of the west, terraced with bleached grey ostrich-eggs of limestone and quartz, to the gentler ridges of the south-east, their pebbles sifted and polished from the debris of ancient glaciers (among them, blood-red jaspers swept down the Irish Sea from the granites of Wicklow and Down). There are agates in the old red sandstone quarried by the waves at the tips of Cork and Kerry headlands; amethyst, still, in the quartzites of Achill; aquamarine in the granite of the Mournes. But, living now above a strand in south-west Mayo, my windowsills are crowded with the different flotsam and jetsam of a sandy shore: sea-urchins, crab shells, bird skulls, the vertebrae of dolphins, their curves instinct with the energy of other lives.

The two kilometres of Thallabawn strand lie open to the Atlantic swells just north of the fiord of Killary Harbour, remote enough from human disturbance to let the otter commute between the waves and the little lakes behind the dunes. Most of the sand is made of shells ground small, so that three-spot cowries, like rolled-up finger-prints, stand out in their wholeness in a shattered mosaic ("the dry shells, the toe- and fingernail parings of the sea" in Michael Longley's image). The tiny fragments are blown across the dunes and rain down onto the flat, grassy machair beyond. Here, their calcium is magically recycled into the shells of abundant land snails, some striped in bright yellows and browns and others the big, dark snails that gardeners know. In winter, long lines of these are wedged into the leeward cracks of driftwood fence-posts in the dunes, their shells sand-blasted to delicate shades of blue.

Rachel Carson, a marine biologist now better remembered for blowing the whistle on pesticides than for her revelatory books about the sea, once tried to buy the only specimen of the lovely, ocean-drifting violet snail *Janthina* in a shell shop in North Carolina. Rebuffed, she waited on luck, and "later I found an empty shell, light as thistledown, resting in a depression in the coral rock of Key Largo, where some gentle tide had laid it". Reading this, I knew her joy, having come upon two of these beautiful, translucent shells, resting within a pace of each other on the tideline. It was a privilege all of a piece with *Janthina's* random lifestyle, since this mollusc travels the surface of the ocean hanging upside down (as we would see it) from a silvery raft made by trapping the wind in bubbles of mucus. It lives on the chance of colliding with, and eating, a little blue jellyfish called *Velella*, or by-the-wind sailor. Sometimes cast up by the million on Ireland's Atlantic shores, this, too, is an ocean drifter, propelled by a little rainbow-coloured sail that it hoists to catch the wind. The odds against snail and jellyfish colliding on the open ocean seem enormous, yet they do this with sufficient frequency to be bonded as predator and prey. When by-the-wind sailors drift ashore, *Janthina* occasionally arrives with them, but snail and jellyfish first meet, far out on the ocean, by bobbing blindly against each other, like toy boats on a park pond.

Infinite chance, infinite time: part of one's pact with the rest of nature is accepting a scale of events quite at odds with our own pell-mell progress. It is a couple of decades since two notable storms, tail-ends of hurricanes, left our strand littered, end to end, with hundreds of washed-up fish. Most were the species from rocky ground out towards the islands – muscular congers, tiny cuckoo wrasse like drifts of pink goldfish, black tadpole fish that no one ever sees. Others we gathered for the freezer: ling, hake, pollack. A scientist friend, a marine biologist, theorised that they had drowned from the shock of sudden change in temperature as masses of water were overturned offshore. Perhaps, but it has never happened since, in any other storm. But a couple of decades is scarcely a flicker on nature's millennial meter, and words like "often" or "rarely" are purely human calibrations. Rarity itself is so often merely a measure of who's around to see.

The more extraordinary events along the shore were once received as part of nature's ordinary chaos, the result of cyclic plagues, random storms, and so on. Today, they are not only more likely to be recorded, but scrutinised for hints of human impact, climate change and altered patterns in the ocean. We no longer feel sure that what we are watching is "natural", and mass strandings and mortalities become runes to be read for the future of the planet. What was to be made of a great winter arrival of cuttle-bones (those oval, chalk-white buoyancy aids at the heart of the squid's inshore cousins)? I had seen very few since my English Channel childhood, yet in 1996 came thousands, swept along the south coast and up the west of Ireland. Two winters later, it was little amber-coloured jellyfish, a pelagic ocean drifter, luminous by night (hence its name, *Pelagia noctiluca*). Arriving by the million, and in every size, it left some beaches glazed in marmalade from Clare to Donegal. In 2007 the same creature, herded around Ireland by winds and currents, fatally enveloped cages of salmon off the Glens of Antrim in enormous, pulsing swarms, ten metres deep and kilometres across.

It is in winter that I go beachcombing most hopefully, sure that a solitary trudge beside the waves must deserve some unusual reward. Wind lifts the sand in long, pale skeins that hiss around my ankles, and leaves flat stones and shells balanced on little mushroom pedestals. Some distant skeins resolve into flocks of sanderling, dunlin or little ringed plovers: miniature waders stirring ahead of me, swirling about, and settling intently in my wake. Turnstones shuffle seaweed in the scribble of the tideline.

Among the weed, abundant plastic, much of it cosmopolitan: French fish-boxes, Canadian milk-crates, Spanish trawlerballs, American lightsticks (fluorescing lures attracting tuna or squid to the baits of long-line hooks). The long-distance items come hairy with hydroids, minuscule animals dressed as ferny plants, or sprout clusters of goose barnacles, nodding on rubbery necks. They all smell intensely of the sea, a dark-green odour whose chemistry shapes the clouds and is thus one of the planet's primal fragrances.

At the furthest reach of the tide, along with the lightsticks, lightbulbs, arms and legs of baby dolls, ubiquitous polypropylene pellets, settles a sparse harvest of tropical drift fruits and seeds – the "sea beans" treasured by generations of beachcombers. Botanically, these are "peregrine disseminules" of jungle vines and bushes. Their arrival on European coasts has been discussed for at least four centuries: the first Irish record of *Entada gigas*, the prominent and robust "sea bean", dates to 1696. "It is very easie to conceive," wrote Hans Sloane, the Irish-born founder of the Chelsea Botanic Garden, "that growing in Jamaica in the woods, they may fall from the Trees into the Rivers, or by any other way conveyed by them into the Sea." He posited a westerly trade wind "for at least two parts of three of the Whole Year, so that the Beans being brought North by the Currents from the Gulf of Florida, are put into these Westerly Winds way and may be supported by this means at last to arrive in [Ireland and] Scotland". Sloane's theory, written when the currents of the oceans were scarcely understood, is strikingly accurate. Perhaps a score of species of tropical plants have seeds capable of staying afloat in salt water for about fourteen months, the least time it takes a small object to drift across to Europe.

Beachcombers are drawn on in unquenchable hope of surprise, its nature happily undefined. In successive winters, years ago, I came upon the eighth and ninth specimens ever found in the world of True's Wonderful Beaked Whale, *Mesoplodon mirus*, rarest of the smaller whales that hunt squid in the deep Atlantic. It was a bumper demonstration of chance, made all the more absurd by hinging on the exact conformation of the animals' two front teeth, its only dentition. This had to be verified, of course, by distant scientific authority, but I was stepping in the sandy footsteps of Frederick William True, an American mammalogist who came upon his prize on a shoal in north Carolina in 1912, and named it "wonderful" in Latin. Nothing so museum-worthy has drifted my way since then, for all my forensic attendance at cetacean remains. Ireland's first *Architeuthis* would be nice: the spectacular giant squid of deep ocean, with tentacles metres long and eyes the size of hub-caps.

The beachcombing naturalist carries two visions of the world in the head, matching mortuary detail to vigorous images of life. In winter, like the fox, and often in its close-stitched footsteps, I wander from one dead seabird to the next, lingering perhaps at one so immaculate and pristine it seems to have closed its eyes the moment before. Where else can I see how the brilliant beak of a puffin grips a whole feed of sandeels for its young, or spread the huge wing of a gannet to feel how it gathers the air? Even the kelp that litters the strand carries in its glistening curlicues the swirl and flow of the undersea forest, the messages sent throbbing landwards twice a day.

Michael Viney, naturalist and writer, lives in Carrigskeewaun, Co Mayo. His acclaimed column, "Another Life", appears weekly in The Irish Times. *His book on life in the West of Ireland,* A Year's Turning, *was published in 1996, followed by* Ireland: A Smithsonian Natural History *in 2003, both from Blackstaff Press. His most recent volume, co-authored with Ethna Viney, is* Ireland's Ocean: A Natural History *(Collins Press, 2008).*

THE ISLAND OF TALKING

Hugo Hamilton

In the steps of Heinrich Böll.

I knew I was crossing a border. Even before they asked me to fasten my seat belt on the way in to Dublin airport, I could feel that I was going across an invisible line. I was back in the island of talking. It's what brings people to life here. We exist in what we say. In Ireland you are nobody unless you're talking, or being talked about, or listening to somebody who is talking about somebody else.

Do borders still matter? I keep asking myself this question. Where does the boundary lie nowadays between countries, between nations, between different forms of culture? I have always lived in those borderlands where things are simultaneously foreign and familiar. I still have one foot in Ireland and one foot in Germany, and maybe the whole idea of identity has become so much more transient now. As a speckled, German-Irish child growing up in Dublin, I must have been asking myself the same question at an early age when I once drew a line with chalk across the kitchen floor and told my mother this was the border between Ireland and Germany. German speakers had to stay on their side and only Irish-speakers were allowed to cross the border into my side. Of course I was merely imitating the way things were done in the adult world, when countries and people were separated from each other along clearly defined lines. My mother laughed. She knew what it was like to be away from home and to live in a foreign country and to look back. She kneeled down and held my hands. With her Rhineland humour she told me that I could not divide up the home like that because otherwise, how could she bake the cake? That made it easier for me to put these childhood obsessions aside. So I rubbed the chalk line away and she got on with the baking.

Perhaps it is impossible to say any more where the boundary lies between different versions of home and belonging. Maybe it's nothing more than a border crossing inside my head. Less fixed than before. Not so easily marked out with chalk. Does anyone need to have a fixed identity any more, or is that an old concept now which applies only to those people who have lost something. Or have we all lost something in the transformation to a more mobile, more "liquid" world. We are more connected, more virtually together in one community, but also more dislocated and less warm-hearted.

So what is it about Ireland that remains unique? If anything, it's not the architecture or the street signs, not the double-yellow parking lines along the kerb, not colour of the buses or the post boxes, not the food or the products on sale in the shops, not even the radio station in the taxi or the DJ's accent, but something in the way that people talk here that is so different. Some natural gift for making connections. Some immediate warmth in their rough, inquisitive talk that creates an instant form of belonging. The gift of including people, the gift of inventing an imaginary, substitute form of home.

On the way in to the city, the streets were full of people in coloured shirts, carrying flags and banners. It was the day of the All-Ireland Final, Cork playing against Galway in the ancient Gaelic game of hurling, the fastest field sport in the world. The crowds had already spilled out over the pavement. The traffic was funnelling slowly through the flooded streets, so I made the quick decision to pay the taxi driver and get out. With my suitcase rolling behind me, I approached Fagan's bar to see if I could get a spare ticket.

"Not a hope", they all said. "The whole world is looking."

I was surrounded by hopeless optimists. I kept running into people who shrugged their shoulders and said they were looking for a ticket themselves. Even the doormen in black suits outside the pub were trying to help. Some Galway girls wearing burgundy T-shirts looked at me with great suspicion and asked me if my suitcase was full of tickets. Some joker in red with "The People's Republic of Cork" written across his chest laughed and said he had a stack of spare tickets at home. Whenever a ticket flashed briefly from the side of a pocket, the lucky holder was pounced on immediately to see if by some a stroke of luck he might somehow part with this precious piece of paper.

People were drinking pints, talking about the traffic on the way up to Dublin, making failsafe arrangements for after the match. Girls laughing like boys, men yelping like girls, elbowing each other as though they couldn't wait for the match to begin. People were forecasting the result, people disappearing in the last minute rush for the toilets, people collecting for Asthma, for the Rossport Five. An old man with a saintly expression held up a placard reading: *Spare ticket for a genuine fan*. And through the middle of all this, a young woman with a child in a buggy parted the crowd like an ambulance with the siren blaring "sorry, sorry".

Further up the street I found two men negotiating over what looked like the last ticket on earth. One of them rushed off in a great hurry, leaving the ticket tout behind holding up his hands. I had come too late.

"Sorry", he said. "He's just gone to the cash machine."

When I asked him out of curiosity how much he was charging for the ticket, he spotted a moment of true opportunism. He must have sensed how eager I was.

"Highest bidder", he said in a more official tone.

He was ready to sell me the ticket quickly for a higher price before the other man returned. But I shook my head. How could I snatch this golden piece of luck from a man who had already agreed a price and was now on his way. I could see him on his way back from the cash machine. The tout instantly changed his mind back again, became an honest trader once more and said he couldn't, in all fairness, sell me a ticket that he had already promised to another punter.

The Irish have always been the world champions at talking, at tea drinking, they have a good claim on alcohol consumption and smoking, even drugs, they have taken up coffee like a new faith, shopping like a new fiction, but above all, they have always been the heroes of optimism and opportunity. The Irish were forced by history to live on their luck. Ireland is perhaps the only country were the national talent of "chancing your arm" has so suddenly led from stagnation to invention, where despair and corruption were turned into high enterprise. It's the only country in the world where a former head of state sued and won a libel action against a newspaper in London for being called a "gombeen man", a unique Irish term for money-lender – a clever sort of provincial, parasitical fool.

Ireland was the country of which the German writer Heinrich Böll said in the 1950s that it remained outside the European social order, where poverty was no disgrace. At least it was not something we ever talked about very much. The Irish landscape is losing its memory now. Most of the ruins of cottages from the post-famine times have been cleared, as if the Irish were determined to erase the signs of poverty from the past. And maybe it is no disgrace for us to be wealthy now and to live in comfortable houses and to distance ourselves from the destitution in our history.

If Ireland has always been the island of talking then it was also the island of not talking and not saying things, the island of talking up a great silence about its own problems. A place where emigration was seen as a natural disaster, like the weather, something you could do nothing about, except to abandon the landscape to those brave enough to stay behind. And maybe it takes a certain amount of prosperity before any country can relax and fully examine the past.

Maybe we still have some catching up to do. The confession box in Ireland has been replaced by the phone-in radio programme. Everybody is eager to talk now, to give the moral guidance which once belonged to the priests. After years of being obsessed with religion and nationalism and sense of place, we have now begun to understand the value of owning things. We mistrust the concept of public space. Even our heritage sometimes gets in the way of our planning aspirations. We have gone from self-denial to self-indulgence, the sociologist Tom Inglis tells us. We have exchanged patriotism for property, religion for consumer dreams.

Ireland – a nation of ticket touts? Of course that's going a bit too far. But it is true that the Irish have begun to believe in their own success, in the man-made environment. They have a reputation for doing business in such a way that it looks like fun to part with your money. Perhaps it is our urge to celebrate, to squander, to meet fate with generosity and affluence.

We remain the great, unstoppable optimists of Europe. We have money in both pockets, as the saying used to go. Every Irish household now has to have an electric sandwich-maker, a tanning bed, and whirlpools and beds with canopies. The stories we tell ourselves now are invented by multinationals like Sony and Debenhams. The Irish have always traded on the fact that they were a people who had things done to them. Governed by abstract forces, by outsiders, by famine, by emigration, by isolation and by lack of resources. More by the Catholic Church and by corrupt politicians. We see ourselves as a people who deserved a break.

We have finally imagined our way out of poverty. We have imagined our way out of the conflict in Northern Ireland. And maybe there is something in the language, in the way we speak to each other that still protects us from the worst. Some lucky twist of humour in the way we express ourselves that saves us from having to look the cold truth of our situation straight in the eye. The former Taoiseach, Bertie Ahern, one of the architects of the Northern Irish peace process and figurehead of the Irish boom years, told a planning tribunal in which his finances were under investigation that the reason he could not remember what he did on a particular date was that he "didn't do it". And Martin McGuinness, just as the Northern Assembly was re-convened and he finally sat down in the power-sharing government with his oldest and fiercest enemy, Ian Paisley, said "this is history like we've never seen it before".

Maybe I was reading too much into the character of a tout. In fact it was me who had become the true opportunist, waiting to see if the tout outside Croke Park stadium might come up with another ticket. The traffic was down to a standstill. The shops were doing a fantastic trade in sandwiches, water, mints. People in the red brick houses were leaning out the windows to watch the surging crowd from above. Sash windows held up by improvisation, by a bottle of sunflower oil, a can of beer, anything that would keep the air coming in on a hot, September afternoon. When the tout eventually found another ticket, he wanted to convince me that he would never double-cross anyone. He was no "gombeen man", in other words, and I had to pay him an extra twenty euros more than the other man before me, because this truly was the last ticket on earth.

Seconds later, I was moving towards the stadium, masquerading as a genuine fan, except for the suitcase rolling behind me, tripping everybody up. There was only one thing to do, to leave it somewhere. But the pubs would not take responsibility. The shops had no space. It was back to shaking heads until I came across a dry cleaners where two girls from the Philippines said they would gladly look after it until the match was over. They refused to accept any money and finally I had become a true fan, slipping through the ratchetting sound of the turnstile, into the Hogan Stand of the all-seater, non-smoking Croke Park stadium.

I was now surrounded by the lucky ones – men, women and children, over eighty thousand people all talking at once, passing around sweets, swapping jokes, speaking across three rows of seats, throwing half-insults across six. Everyone had an attitude, an accent, a coloured cowboy hat, scarf, flag or woollen bracelet. Everybody sizing each other up, running down the opposition, listening to the ring of triangles coming from the brass band, waiting for the President of Ireland to walk out on the red carpet and shake hands with the players.

"Who are you up for?" the man beside me asked. He wanted to know what he was dealing with and whether I was on his side, for Galway. I gave a neutral answer and he gave me a dubious look, as though a man without conviction was not to be trusted, even less than the opposition. Men coming in at the last minute turned to look all around saying: "Who are we stuck with? God help us, they're all Cork around here". One of them pointed at me and accused me of being a Cork man in disguise, making the man beside me even more suspicious. Then a woman three seats away to my left leaned over and asked me if I was related to Eleanor Murphy.

Eleanor Murphy, no, not that I was aware of. I shook my head and she examined me as though I was denying something.

"Do you mind me asking you a question?" she said.

"Of course", I nodded.

"Where did you get your ticket?"

Suddenly I felt like an impostor. In front eighty two thousand fans who had come to watch the final, sell-out match of this enduring amateur sport, I was forced to admit that I had bought the last ticket on earth from a tout.

"Just as I thought", she smiled.

But she was not blaming me, as it turned out. On the contrary, her accusation turned into a form of inclusion. She could fully understand how a man would become so desperate. She explained that she was in charge of the tickets for that entire row of seats. They had come from a Canadian hurling club and my ticket had been sold to a woman by the name of Eleanor Murphy who "swore to God" that it was a gift for her nephew who was stone mad about hurling but had now betrayed the game by "scurrilously" selling it for profit. She thanked me for helping to uncover a great fraud.

The noise level lifted and the game got under way at last. I wondered if the hidden German inside me could ever fully understand the rules. To semi-foreign eyes it still appears like a form of marital arts with wooden sticks, arm extensions with which the players, some with cages around their heads and some without, scooped the *sliotar* (ball) off the grass and whacked it up the field. There was a clack every time the hurley connected with this clump of solid leather, sending it into the air like a shot from a gun and sending tremors all the way back through the player's arms, ribs, legs, right into his groin.

Along the sideline, there were stewards carrying dozens of new, replacement hurleys, for whenever a player broke one on the field and held it up in the air like a fractured limb. Sometimes the referee took down a name for foul play, but it was not always easy to distinguish between foul play and good play, when players were shouldering each other, when blood flowed occasionally, when hurleys clashed like swords and a hand came up in the middle of it all to snatch the ball out of the air. The trick seemed to be in the way that a player twisted and turned, the rabbit-like intuition with which he could send an opponent the wrong way and run free with the ball on top of the hurley like a spontaneous egg and spoon race.

In Connemara, where there were very few trees and no level fields, only rocky patches of green, the children used to play on the beach with hurleys made of seaweed. Hurling is a game, they tell me, that was originally played without any referee, only a code of honour in which the players reminded each other of the rules. And there were legendary games without any rules at all, such as the one that took place once on the beach around Christmas on the Great Blasket, where the men fought each other with sticks until the winning team finally drove the other team into the sea.

The game in Croke Park had become more civilized. Every time Cork scored a point, a man behind me roared the word "HUR. . .LING" like an elongated cry at the top of his voice.

When a Galway player scored, the man beside me waved his programme in front of my face, pointing at the player's photograph, saying that he was a genius and "still" only twenty-two years of age.

At half time, with the score almost level, Sharon Shannon came out on the field to play her accordion and increase the tension with a polka. The crowd became even more noisy for the second half. When Galway scored a goal, the entire stadium rose to its feet, shouting and waving anything they could. Men were drumming their feet on the seats. The man beside me kissed his programme. A father held up a two-year-old boy in the air over his head. Somebody tried to sing "The West Awake" but was drowned out by the roar.

Galway played with great fire, but in the end it was all Cork. In fact, they could have driven the Galway players into the sea, but then the final whistle blew and the players dropped their tired hurleys, threw head cages in the air, shook hands and embraced each other. A crowd ran out on the pitch to touch the winners, to get autographs written on their backs, to carry players shoulder high toward the winning stand. After a number of short announcements, a priest stepped up to present the cup and to speak a few words with equal affection for the winners and the losers.

The Cork captain, Seán Óg Ó hAilpín, held the cup in the air for the cheering crowd and made a speech, still out of breath from the action on the field. And maybe it added to the power of the event that he spoke in fluent Irish, though he was actually born in Fiji, that his mother was from Fiji and that his father was Irish. In other words, that he, too, was speckled like me, living in the cultural borderlands between two identities, though without question, far more athletic and courageous than myself.

The woman who had unmasked me as an impostor said he was extremely handsome, "even though he's from Cork". On the big screen above the crowd, I could see that she was probably right – he had an inch-long duelling scar across the top of his left cheek.

On the narrow streets outside the stadium, the crowds walked past the front windows of the houses, talking and laughing, their voices surely penetrating right through the rooms into the back. The pubs were already overflowing and people were now predicting the number of pints they were going to drink. I heard a man saying that he was going to murder a big steak. Another man saying he would "fuckin" murder a sushi, anything at all that was edible, he was so hungry. He would even eat the hand that feeds him. People found each other at street corners, outside the undertakers, at the Lady Luck take-away. People describing their exact location on mobile phones while they were only yards away from each other and merely had to turn around to meet face to face. And everywhere the chance meetings between past pupils, past lovers, relatives, friends who hadn't seen each other in years, accidentally running into each other on the streets of Dublin.

I made my way into the city, past Fay's Dancing Shoes, past the Express Denture Clinic. Pigeons sat in neat rows on the roof of a house, like silent, defeated hurling supporters, waiting to see what the crowd might eventually leave behind. As I turned into Gardener Street, to where the Novenas are still being held each year in the Church of Saint Francis Xavier, it struck me that the only priest I had seen so far was at Croke Park, presenting the trophy. I had not laid eyes on a single nun. The priests who were seen on every street fifty years ago addressing people as "my child", were nowhere to be found. The only people to be seen in black suits now were the bouncers standing outside Dublin pubs. And the faithful flock which had once knelt down spontaneously in the streets for the Angelus bell had also disappeared. Instead, the country was talking itself up into a bright new future, leaving everything behind in the past. I was walking through the last enclave of Irish Catholicism, past the Marian Bed and Breakfast, past the Fatima Bed and Breakfast, past the suppliers of liturgical metals with tiered brass candle-holders, down into a city converted to the secular world.

The extract above was first published in German as the opening chapter of Die Redselige Insel *(Luchterhand Verlag, 2007), a travel book in which Hugo Hamilton retraced the Irish travels of Heinrich Böll, a half century after his renowned travelogue* Irisches Tagebuch (Irish Journal).

Hugo Hamilton was born in Dublin in 1953, of Irish-German parentage. He is the author one collection of short stories and six novels, most recently Disguise *(Fourth Estate, 2008). He has also published an acclaimed memoir of his Irish-German childhood,* The Speckled People *(Fourth Estate, 2003), and a sequel,* The Sailor in the Wardrobe *(Fourth Estate, 2006). He lives in Dublin.*

WRITING OUT THE MYTH

John F. Deane

Locus iste . . .

Anton Bruckner, quiet-spoken, faith-inclined, sat
in his drawing-room assembling
harmonies, "*vierstimmigen Chor*" – motets, music

to penetrate the soul with its seduction, sacred
fountains of the love of God: *locus iste*
a Deo factus est in aestimabile sacramentum;

a priceless sacrament . . .

*

This is the morning flight, the Irish on the move,
different migrations now out over Holyhead;
a still, a scarcely tiding, Irish Sea of clouds

and England's pleasing pasturelands. Take a right
turn south, banking; gleams from a car six miles below;
old Europe, the fabulous, we breast-stroke through

blue lakes of air, in over Amsterdam (Anne Frank),
and Leipzig (Bach's *Thomaskirche*), Prague (Franz Kafka)
towards Budapest (and Attila József), and at last

(Warsaw, Dresden, should we drift a little to the north)
down the long slope of air into Sofia, new world,
international wolves of promise

moving down out of Vitosha's snow-patched peaks.
Then see me rise, in a luxe glass cage, with garrulous writers
on the outside wall of a plush, post-communist, hotel.

*

Father's handwriting was a fishing-line
shivering in the chill air;
it sloped forward, dangerously, in a haste
to catch up on the words

shoaling across his brain;
he left small
translations, exclamations, tracks,
on the margins of his books so I could hear

the snorting horses of Taras Bulba
gallop over the steppes
of Bunnacurry bogs.
Towards the end it was squiggle-writing,

tapering off at last
as if a fly, rambling across spilled blue ink,
had at last lifted off the earth
into thin air, into pure air, into Word.

*

Sofia: the heavy-set, vast and rough-old-times
Palace of Culture where we come, coralled together
to fret about indifference to our words: heavy-set

serious men and women, Azerbaijan to the USA
spilling out words on words across the floor, bland
marble playthings, the world beyond beyond us.

*

In the beginning I had crayons,
waxy, thick as my father's middle finger;
paper from old brown packaging;

I made lines, my every-which-way
rush across the earth, my marks,
my lightning-flashes, slug-trails.

*

Mausoleum hall, Sofia; I return my earpiece and translation set
and make my way to the table, wines and meats, more un-
animated conversation. I have come a long way

from island. Or have I? Afternoon, see us, European
Academy of poetry, Luxembourg, Slovakia, handling
strange languages in tangle-weeds of words.

*

I had a slate before me on the desk
where I slid in,
short pants, short legs; a pristine finger

of white chalk.
I made a line, waverful, a scratching,
like hens; Mrs Kilbane applauded:

"you have written – I!"
I had a pen, at a big desk, a brass
sliding-lid over a depthless well of sea-blue ink,

had a headline copybook: *Pim put a bib on Bab*
with a pin:
and soon it will be joined-up

writing; I will be part of it, a link in the Altamira chain
through Achill Island
to Zimbabwe. The word. The Word.

Joined-up signs, in order,
like vine-rows on the hills of Aquitaine,
like fence-posts

driven down to keep the lifestock safe;
(Pats Larry,
when Mrs Kilbane was out,

dug the nib down
in the wood of the desk, as if the words
were iron tines, I knew he was digging in

for trouble,
that broken nib, timber of the pen snapped off
like twigs;)

I still write down the word, the pronoun, with the same
waverful scratching feel, knowing I have never
got it right, the same word, the word: "I".

*

Off the marsh road, a flock of stray and vagrant
    high-stepping cranes, grave demoiselles, has been moving
        in slow ballet across the wet

as if the earth on which they deigned to walk
    were tarnished, tarnishing and giving life. They have become
        travellers, winds taking them from their natural

environment. We know, too, how storms take us, set us down
on unknown territory where we grasp for hold.
Paul, the apostle, told how he was lifted off the earth

and into Paradise, discovering things of which
no one might speak;
I have been listening now, for decades; moments

when I achieve a sacred quiet, I have heard
with Bruckner, Elgar, Brahms, harmonies
beyond listening; I have been offered words and set

them down, relishing a slow, muted applause,
yours John Donne, George Herbert's, yours
Hopkins, and yours, Andrew Marvell. I listen

where the full-dressed poplar down by the red gate
sashays silkily in its obligation; I set it down
defiantly, in your shadow, Dickinson, at your side, Smart.

Mist this morning on the still grasses. The spiders' webs
– slight as dream-catchers – scarcely visible
on bush and heather, shiver

wispfully in the no-breeze; an old man, gaunt
in the inheritance of famine, has lost his son
to the murk of a canal and walks his rush-snagged fields,

in silence, eyes dulled as daub. I am relearning
ignorance so I may write foolishly again and say
it will be all right, it will be all

right; we carry inside our flesh the bones
of the death of the Lord Jesus
and on our shoulder-blades the nubs

of spirit-wings. Paul
    could never tell for sure, whether his flight
        was in or out of body. And always

Icarus stands aggrieved, waxwings raised
    in preparation for the myth, listening for the breeze
        that will lift him out of flesh into the gorgeous sun.

*

In the rich plains of Bulgaria there are sudden
acres of poppies, blood-red sheets against the yellow
fields of corn; and here and there

small hills of discarded tyres, factory complexes
abandoned to stonefall and weed-growth;
at our conference, the big men listen to their own voices

saying I am big, important, cover my chest
with medals and walk behind me at respectful distances,
dark-clothed, dark-fleshed, and aggrieved, sophisticated men.

*

In his drawing-room, Anton Bruckner sat,
wearied, knowing
his Symphony No. 9 in D Minor
would not be finished:

he was sitting by the window, allowing darkness;
a few last rooks
crossed, black against grey, towards the wood;
he was there not-there, thinking

thinking how his symphony might close with a chorus –
Freude, D Major,
like his master's, how he had worked to put
the self-rending God

together again: all the king's horses, all the king's men. . .
He laughed, his own *Te Deum*
ranging through his mind. Now, about his grave,
mother-of-pearl dragonflies are shivering in sunlight.

*

There remains
a heart-light, one
you will not declare at the borders,
nor flash
at passport control: your will to live

justly, without despair,
your will to offer
mercy, to accept forgiveness,
your will to walk
with hope, without expectation, in the shadow

of your urgent God
and to express, in the moments
offered to you on this one and insulated day,
the sentences
you have been entrusted to translate:

John F. Deane was born in 1943 on Achill Island, Co Mayo. He is the author of two novels and nine collections of poetry, most recently The Instruments of Art *(2005) and* A Little Book of Hours *(2008), both from Carcanet Press. In 1979, he founded Poetry Ireland, the national poetry organization, and* Poetry Ireland Review. *He lives in Dublin.*

TWO POEMS

Leontia Flynn

OUR FATHERS

for Nicky Carey

Our fathers,
the first gigantic men
of the earth – our teachers –
have, at the end,

become creatures,
almost, of air.
What anchors
them (my father's hair

is thistledown,
his smile the slow
swoop of a distant bird, blown
over his body) to now

and to here?
A radar blip
in the darkness; the last flare
fired at sea; the snap

and pop of a synapse
crossed – closing
its spaces . . . and perhaps
he'll weigh in

– hello! – my father,
tethered,
for a bit, by the
least thing. Talk of the weather

is one; laughter
which follows punchlines,
nods – nudge nudge – a handshake:
these are signs

and our calendar
customs – our days, months, weeks,
these are brail
or a trail

of breadcrumbs –
or rosary beads
in his hands (all thumbs)
by which – yes indeed –

we seek to delay
them, our fathers. The fire
is lit. "Stay"
we say, "pull up a chair,"

thinking – heh heh – if we can trap
them,
then we can keep
them,

and if we can keep them
– we'll keep them . . . forever!!!
But my father
my father

my father holds open
the door of himself
and lets his old ghost
pass through

before him
("after you, after you"
He mouths): his guest,
– his old self – stealth

-ily tip
-toeing out (Shhh)
– one finger on his lips –
leaving only the hush

". . ."
of evening – falling
on the households,
– creaking and settling –

of a generation:
on their thresholds
of pain and love – Amen, Amen
on the townlands.

On the white fields

SPRING POEM

When, in morning light, I walked to the bridge
– that old skeleton propped on ribs of steel –
I thought of my dead father;
but neither his loss, my pain, or near dispersal
into competing selves which flew past others,
drove me to the edge.

Neither this nor thinking of lost autumn nights,
cool and comforting, like when I was a child
and drew up the bed sheets;
or even – horror – the early, creeping signs
under the eaves and round the colonnades
of growing things;

no, none of this spurred to spring or swallow dive
over the railing, into the abyss
and there begin again;
as every fall, through meaning and its loss,
lets us begin: as *live* becomes *believe* –
in love, oblivion.

Leontia Flynn was born in 1973 in Belfast and attended Queen's University Belfast and the University of Edinburgh. Her first collection, These Days *(Cape), appeared in 2004, and a second,* Drives, *also from Cape, in late 2008. She is currently Research Fellow at the Seamus Heaney Centre for Poetry, Queen's University Belfast.*

ESSAY AND POEMS

Aidan Carl Mathews

THE SKIN OF OUR TEETH

Out of the saline tumult of things,
this green, painful life.

–Once upon a time, I say, a man was living happily ever after.

–That's not a story, the child says. Tell me a story with a story in it.

–It has a beginning, I tell her. It has an ending. It has a man in the middle of his sentence.

But she runs off in disgust and so, on an ordinary day unlike any other, I can turn on the television as the Angelus rings in the six o'clock news. Ads for toothpaste on one channel; flies on an African face on another; on a twiddled third the beestung lips of a singer pleading her platinum heartbreak. There are fourteen stations on my set, and I sit in the lotus with my slimline remote control, like an Emperor at the Colosseum thumbing through a checklist of doomed contestants as they slaughter each other between the commercials, for the whole world's woes are a spectator-sport to the couch-potato. Here's a rapist running under a macintosh into a Black Maria as a carbonated fruitjuice pleasures my taste-buds; and now a boy with a belt-drive weapon poses proudly among mortar-shells and sacks of flour for the international press as I break hard chocolate in its sugar casing on the two back teeth that supermodels sacrifice to achieve a fluted contour in the cheek-bone. In a word, I am home again, home again.

And then there is a knock on the door. Now a knock on the door is the most terrible expression in the English language, and it must be worse in the languages of Eastern Europe and worst of all perhaps in the tongues of the two great civilisations of Germany and Russia. If Yiddish, the language that went on praying and praising between them, between Germanic and Slavic speech, were itself still spoken in Europe, a knock on the door would resound through the woodpulp paper of its dying dictionary. The pages would scatter in all directions like leaves in a cemetery when a gale-force wind vandalises the lindens.

But this is not a militiaman's truncheon rat-tat-tapping the spyhole. Not the bad Beethoven's Fifth of a fist hammering hard; not the circumspect rapping of doorsteppers; not a jogger with the census forms whose eau-de-cologne you inhale as you tell her your wife is the real head of the household; nor the age-old old-age pensioner with her updated issue of *The Watchtower* who makes you wonder what the world has done to her that she wants it to end on such a beautiful evening, all swallows and the vapour-trails of airplanes; not a jobless woman with a bootleg jokebook or a man raffling weekends in the West of Ireland for motor neuron disease, for muscular dystrophy, for cystic fibrosis, for the sake of a bedridden child, from the sight of a terminal wife. It is instead a very timid knocking of the knuckle of one finger on the stained glass panel where a Jew would hang verses from Deuteronomy in a little metal canister.

Bone of my bone, flesh of my flesh, it is my own child, my first born, on the doorstep. She stands in her bicycle helmet, her shorts and sneakers, with a look of great bafflement on her eight-year-old face, as if I were a new word she had never come across before, as if she was unsure how to pronounce me, as if I were written in reverse like the Hebrew for life.

–Jesus Christ, I say.

Her lips are broken back and burst open like plums. Her mouth is a violet hole, a running cavity. Long teeth dangle from her gums on slick threads of tissue, like seeds from the pink strings of a gouged watermelon. Blood gargles over the jawstrap of her helmet, over the pound-shop choker at her throat. It is all downhill from there like the law of gravity. It has even spotted her trainers like poster paint. It is all uphill from here like the gravity of the law.

When she sees the horror set in my face, it rises in hers. I lift her over the doorstep, over the sudden threshold, as if there were a wave about to slam its green gallons against her. I take her up into my arms because I cannot bear to look at her. I cannot bear to look at this image of her likeness. And all the decent words which are the prerogative of lovers at the crisis of their passion regurgitate in my throat as the doggerel of rage.

–Anything up? says my wife from the kitchen, from the jelly settling slowly in the mould of a sea-shell, from the school copybooks piled in an obelisk on the table where the candle is already lighting for our breaking of bread. Inside in the living room the baby is playing with the stations in search of the children's channel.

It's time for evening prayer, and perhaps there's someone reading it in the stationary lanes where we're stalled among the trucks and the hatchbacks in the stricken short cuts of the way to hospital. Over to one side in the frozen slipstream there's a chap flossing his teeth at the rear view mirror, snarling and screwing up his face the way a toddler does from the bored back seat at the driver behind him; away on the right, a girl in glasses is stencilling her lips with the pastels of arousal. But there's probably someone within two sets of lights who has the prayerbook open on the steering wheel, its pages sticky from a soggy mandarin.

–Lord, open our lips

–And we shall praise your name.

I prayed it myself this morning on the motorway, sitting in traffic with the window down, tapping the hairs from my shaver out onto the double yellow lines, because the distance from my home to my work is a sabbath day's journey, just right for a midtempo recitation. And why not? The Dublin to Wexford road is as good as Galilee for honouring the God of all our goatpaths. If the amber's with you, you can finish the intercessions in the car-park; if the blockage is bad, you can search among the traumas on the medium wave for some rhythm and blues to bolster your sunrise in the few free minutes left. But it's always there in its limp red jacket, the bittersweet psalter like a punnet full of wild honey to restore my hunger in a season of sweeteners. It offers sodality and solidarity with those in the longitude of Greenwich mean-time, or any other time zone in the two hemispheres, who desire to celebrate the clockface of eternity, and it offers comradeship as well with those who don't or can't or won't and wouldn't do so. Christians and post-Christians and non-Christians are living the psalms out loud as I read them to myself without moving my lips; and the daylight saving of my pat devotions doesn't hold a candle to the *aurora borealis* of their struggle and their stamina.

My wife presses the horn like an air-raid siren. Now the van in front of her drives more slowly. The cars around us close ranks to rebuke her. – I love you, I say to the head of hair on my shoulder. The goo on my shirt, glue and mucus, a shiny streel of it, glosses and matts the buttondown collar; bad breath like a baby's croup pants on my skin. – I love you, I say. I love you more than anyone. I love you more than your sister. I love you more than your mummy. And the head of hair nods and nods until I tell her not to, not to, because I'm afraid she'll asphyxiate on her own gristle, on the debris where her lips were opened by handlebars and a granite gatepost.

–Don't speak, I tell her. Say nothing. Say nothing at all. It'll only make it worse. I promise.

This morning when the sun was blinding the other side of the supermarket, laminating the trolleys, rank upon rank of them at the automatic doors, I sat in my Starlet chanting verses from the Book of Daniel, from the canticle of acclamation sung by the three just men in the furnace; but you do not sing with one voice in the heart of a fire. You do not sing at all. And I can imagine myself among the sophomores of Capernaum, like a modern seminarian with his Barth and his Balthazar, crouched at the ankles of the yogi, the charismatic hasid from Nazareth, breathless with the depth and decompression of his tutorial, my head swirling with Talmud Torah and talk of the Kingdom and the bad air of a sunken room that's packed with people – and suddenly the sky collapses, the roof crashes in, and the stench of a palliasse, the sight of a stick insect on a plank, levered in, lowered down, scatters all our theology, as four pairs of hands – four gospels you might say – open up the heavens to reveal crucified human nature, *homo ex machina*, as the new dove over a new baptism.

–We're here, she says. We're there.

My wife parks in the handicapped space and the doors open before us like the curtains of a theatre as we run towards them, breaking their beam of light.

He's a young doctor. Young enough to have the stethoscope sticking out of his pocket. He uses his hands like a chaplain, like he's signing in the language of the deaf and the dumb.

–You're a great old girl, he keeps saying. A great old girl. Open your lips, love.

And she is great. Great and old. She's passed through a tiny seam in the universe, through twenty past six on an autumn evening, a harvest night, a full moon, and now she's deeper in the world, deeper in the mystery, the taste of apple on her tonsils yielding to the taste of wine, the taste of wine to the dull sulphur smell of her own blood.

–Thirty across, says the teenage boy on the bench beneath the No Smoking sign. Relating to the female, OK? Four letters ending in -unt, OK?

–Grunt, says his friend.

–Jaysus, the teenage boy says. That's five.

–You have to tell us, says the Casualty Officer with the cheloid scar on his throat. You have to tell us exactly what you took.

But the addict stares at the ceiling of the Accident and Emergency as if it were the Planetarium, and says nothing. He is lying on his back, holding his stomach the way a pregnant woman would, her fingers spread on the trampoline of her belly, feeling the spring of the step inside her.

–You want to die? says the Casualty Officer. – Is that it? You want the whole world to carry your coffin?

They have winched the curtains across at the next cubicle while a houseman beats on a pensioner's chest like a door or as if he were trying to stamp shut the lid of a trunk that's too full. In the gingham pleats of the plastic I can see the silhouette of his wife, the wings of her glasses, blur of her torso, as she sits still, not making a sound.

–I'm bursting to go, says a nurse beside me. I have to greet the seat. Give me three minutes. And off she goes, with the chatty wristwatch pinned to the brown of her breast, time and eternity. But which is which?

–Aunt, you eejit, says the teenage boy with the tabloid crossword. –Aunt. And they laugh until they cry.

–Thank God it's her first teeth, says the doctor with the stethoscope. He is swabbing and staunching, scooping the cuttlefish fragments out of the wet oedema of her wound, for the bone above the teeth is crushed and the mouth puffed like a bullet hole. When she was little she kissed me on the lips; nowadays she kisses me on the cheeks; when I'm old and demented in a commode wheelchair, using my remote control as a mobile phone to ring my dead father, she'll kiss me on the forehead and cry in the corridor.

–They're her second teeth, my wife says. She's had four since Easter.

The addict slews by me on a gleaming trolley; his eyes are squinting to make them out, the starbursts he can see from the bridge of his journey. And the cubicle curtains roll back to reveal a brand-new widow whose husband is not here among the living and the dying. In a moment she will be offered a cup of tea, with or without sugar, and someone will ring the neighbours. Otherwise the rack of lamb in the oven will burn down the house. And the porter will push the body down the corduroys of the ramp to the mortuary and label the toe that a hand sprinkled with talcum powder twelve hours ago. As he loops the tag to knot it, some baby's wrist in another corridor of the complex will be given its own disposable plastic cuff with the name and date of delivery on it. The same florist will service both orders, casket and crib. And tonight, when the newborn's belching milk, the torso on the slab will vent its airlock in a bullfrog's croaking.

I lean over the mess of her mouth as the doctor chooses among his suture needles like fishing tackle.

–Try not to say anything, I tell her. Try not to try.

–Daddy, she says. I am a little girl.

It is the first time she has spoken. She has taken the words out of my mouth.

–Speak to me, says the casualty officer to the man who has swallowed pills, paraquat or whatever. Speak to me for God's sake. And the widow of two and a half minutes has begun to cry in a shy, sly, stifled way, out of consideration for everyone else in this domain of body odours and dettol, this Accident and Emergency room.

–Ssshh, my wife says, stroking her hair as tiny tears spurt from the tip of the doctor's syringe. Ssshh. In the awful overhead light my wife's face is almost as old as her hands.

I have never been sure of the cul-de-sac where I live. Is it a keyhole or a hammerhead? Children play among sycamore seeds in its tarred centre; adults watch from a lace vigil, from doors whose letter-boxes and lock-barrels are wired for thieves. Christ to the left of me; Christ to the right of me: every species of human genius may be found here, the breakdowns, the break-ups, the breakthroughs, the oxygen and leaf-fall of my lovely deciduous kind, Eden and Gethsemane in one, unison, harmony and counterpoint, the agile, killing pilgrimages of our individual stories. God's plenty, God's people, multiply and increase here in the green sequence of their dramas beyond Sophocles, beyond Shakespeare, beyond the baroque obesity of breakfast television. Within a mile of me the whole topography of Palestine folds and unfolds: Jerusalem and the Jordan, the footbridges, flyovers, ringroads and zebra crossings of a holy people in a holy place. And tonight as the boy with cerebral palsy turns in a figure of eight among the eucalyptus in his new motorized wheelchair, and the separated dad watches the clock while his daughters drink their milkshakes in the lifeboat in MacDonald's, the children of my road are prospecting the ground at their feet, like Hansel and Gretel groping in the undergrowth for the pebbles that will lead them home again, home again. They are searching by torchlight for teeth in the gravel; and when they find them, they will carry them in a tiny Maguire and Paterson matchbox, the two red almonds, to the hospital on the hill. The doctor will bed them like bulbs in the sluice of her gums; and watch and wait, and watch and wait again, and weigh it all up in a day, a week, a month of Sundays. They may take; they may thrive: it's happened before. It'll happen again. The mouth is amazing. *Orate. Oremus.*

–You must hold them in with your hands, he says. At the right angle, the right aim, the right pressure. If they slip and slide out, there's no point. The tooth and the tissue have to be wedded. But you must understand – and he glances at the child on the trolley that's marked "Property of the Hospital" in indelible black ink because he doesn't want her to understand what's he's saying. You must understand that the probability calculus in this instance is pretty deplorable.

My daughter is staring at the ceiling like the addict stared, like the widow stared at the floor with its sheen of industrial cleanser; she's staring at it as if she could see angels ascending and descending in the climax and anticlimax of revelation; and because she's mine, because I can trace my descent from her, because she brought me into the world when I was twenty nine and she was already as old as homo sapiens, and because she's a starchild, an incarnation, her body radioactive with traces of the heaviest elements on the periodic table, the enormous atoms that were constituted in the first three minutes of the universe, and because her mother went barefoot into her room, as if it were a mosque for minors, to stash a pound coin under a pillow when her first milk teeth melted, I want to ask why. Because is a question; and why is the only answer.

–How long do I hold them in? my wife says. She has cut her nails already while I was thinking. Her lap is full of plain parings.

–Until the morning, says the doctor. Say twelve hours. And then as long as you can keep going.

–Show me what to do and I'll do it, she says. She has tugged her engagement ring from a hand that smells of chalk and kitchen gloves and she's slipping it on the child's first finger.

–It could be worse, the doctor tells her. You can see for yourself. And he heads a ball with his perfect crease towards the midfield of the night's admissions.

Of course it could. It could be the child in the Pine Forest with the poor face full of silicone and scar tissue, or the anorexic with her cache of laxatives under the collapsible Christmas tree in the attic; it could be the boy in a private room whose sister has been reading him newsagent novels, full of brothels and Gestapo, and he still won't wake from his spaghetti junction of drips and monitors, from his fourth-day coma; or the quadriplegic whose voyages would intimidate Christopher Columbus, his mattress rising and settling in its slow rotary see-saw like the flotsam of a raft. It could even be the woman with the haemorrhage in the story of Jairus and his daughter, or Jairus and his daughter in the story of the woman with the haemorrhage. Whose story is it, after all, in the diagonal agenda of that tale, in that intersecting text where each element of the narrative is both subplot and centrepiece, where chronicle and anecdote exist in dialogue and dialectic? For Jairus is a personage, a potentate, an eloquent and estimable senior member of synagogue, and his prostration at the feet of Jesus ostentatiously ratifies the controversial standing of a *zaddik* whose own family refuses to authorise him. Everything here is urgency, emergency, the shaman and the showman striding ahead of the multitudes in the dustcloud of their pandemonium toward the sickbed of a child in a pubertal stupor. For the billboards and the bulletins this is hard copy, real news, the gospel truth of the day's tidings. The more highly valued the sufferer, the more highly visible his afflictions. Jairus has the exponential prestige of holiness and affluence, of bank and rank. No wonder the proletariat of his district crowd toward his solid accommodation, toward the caterwauling vaudeville of a bolt out of the blue.

But Jesus is not a televangelist; he is the crucified Christ of faith; and the photo-opportunities – Brokenhearted Bigshot Sees Dead Daughter Dance – are all spectacle and no lens. Clear the house. Family only. Up you get, pet. Now eat something. There is to be no more melodrama: sentimentality is only cruelty in its cups. Authentic anguish merits more than reportage; it deserves a story. It's to the woman at the menopause and not to the girl at the menarche that Jesus turns: it's the presence on the periphery he calls "daughter", not the cherished child around whose fainting fit silly wailing resounds. Some undiscovered, undisclosed immensity of patience exists in his noisy vicinity. He can sense its duration, its endurance.

It touches him. He weakens towards it, towards her. This is no freak lightning strike, no cataclysmic voltage savagely disfiguring bystanders in the trial by ordeal beloved of tabloids or the snap suffering that has all of Jairus' household ululating. This is as inscrutable as daylight; it is the everyday drizzle of the state of pain, of the ongoing, of the undergone, of age and damage, an endless oozing prolapse, eternal internal bleeding.

So within the fake healing of one narrative there occurs the faith healing of another: the girl who was thought to be dead is alive; the woman who was thought to be well is chronically ill. And I sit in the amazement of tears in a general hospital, wondering how many persons with haemorrhages I have passed since I last changed my shirt.

I'm back in the car; an exhausted, creeping bundle twitches on my lap. We're going home again, home again; and I'm trying to make sense of the nonsense. All I do, of course, is make nonsense of the sense.

Injury to the face depends on gender. This is what I say to myself in my fugue. On a boy stigmata, on a girl a stigma. Marks of conflict strengthen the mystique of a male face; or can do. Look at John of the Golden Mouth, my wing-forward schoolfellow with his nine-carat beam. Blemishes in a girl are another matter. They are not testimonials, attributes of strength. They are infirmities. I think of the hare-lip, the cleft palate, the deep design of the final stages of foetal development when the upper lip and the soft tissue under the nostrils merge in a Cupid's bow, and the child is ready to be born.

I think of dentists, of orthodontists, of seatbacks tilted under arc-lights like a birthing chair, of a masked man with thin hair and a thick beard reading the X-ray of my mouth at the wooden louvres of a window in California. I'm still agape, albed in a surgical sheet and bloody, my tongue lungeing like a holy communicant in the dim days of my infancy at the scent of linen and tobacco on the hands of the curate when he laid *Corpus Christi*, the corpse of Christ, in the sterilised vault of my face and I'd breathe through my nose like the God of Genesis so as not to disturb the chapel of repose where I would later chew hairy bacon.

–Theologians should consider the mouth, the dentist says. The whole history of the species is there: the hunter, the carnivore, the flesh-eater. It's all predation. Of course we won't go near the gift-horse because we want to believe we're the donkey that carried Jesus into Jerusalem. The four horsemen know better. Human nature is a story with teeth. No wonder the dominant civilisation can laugh loudest and longest. Look at the size of our incisors.

I see an old man dancing in a pub in Kerry. I haven't thought of him for years. He brandishes his dentures and snaps them like castanets as he twirls at the pool table. Everyone claps; I'm there among them, clapping too. But the middle-aged woman who drops her butts in an empty bottle beside me has steepled her hands to hide her face while she talks, because she's forgotten to put in her plate. How do you move from one to the other, from the shame to the dance, from timidity to bravado except through the demobilisation of age? The ember years are an aftermath, an amnesty almost; and yet a Skid Row senior sleeping in a pre-cast drainpipe in a children's adventure playground in San Francisco sought out the Redwood City student who'd sketched him in charcoal and asked him to work in a good set of teeth. So, back in America, I return to smiling the eighteenth-century smile of reason, of good-humoured gravity, because the students parade their ivories in a trophy glow like Mormons, and I can't match the moonshine.

–You can buy teeth at a roadside stall in India, the dentist says. I kid you not. I have pictures. Couple of rupees. You can haggle for molars, but not in English. They babble like Babel. Of course, American Express is Hello and Goodbye in any language.

And I want to tell him that, no, the mouth is blessing and benediction, it's grace and generosity, that a prostitute will let a john sublet her armpits, her pelvis, her sex, but the mouth is special, is sacred, an alcove for the vowels of love; that the kiss of Judas sets our teeth on edge because it's lipservice and claptrap, and that the child in the serum of the womb, listening to the deep spondees of her mother's heartbeat, its groundbass budding and blooming with the months until it booms like the bell of Notre Dame, will suck her thumb for comfort, for consolation, because the mouth is the focus of all affective life, of nourishment, of laughter and language, of bodies bonded in the enchantment of speech, in the chanting of liturgy, in the sing-song of-small talk, in the profound adventures of trachea and uvula and diaphragm; and I want to tell him that the mother in her labour, as she continues the vast apostolic succession of flesh and blood, of one body squeezed from another in an unbroken chain of heroic human brokenness that stretches and strains back to the very beginning, to a site where our speechless and unspeaking ancestors await the *Parousia* in their prehistoric

A JOURNAL OF CONTEMPORARY WRITING

IRISH PAGES

Outstanding Writing from Ireland and Overseas

Edited in Belfast

IRISH PAGES

IRISH PAGES is a biannual journal, edited in Belfast and publishing, in equal measure, writing from Ireland and overseas.

Its policy is to publish poetry, short fiction, essays, creative non-fiction, memoir, essay reviews, nature-writing, translated work, literary journalism, and other autobiographical, historical, religious and scientific writing of literary distinction. There are no standard reviews or narrowly academic articles. Irish Language and Ulster Scots writing are published in the original, with English translations or glosses.

Each issue includes a number of regular features: *The View from the Linen Hall*, an editorial commenting on cultural or political issues in Ireland or overseas; *From the Irish Archive*, an extract of writing from a non-contemporary Irish writer, accompanied by a brief biographical note; *In Other Words*, a selection of translated work from a particular country; and *The Publishing Scene*, a commissioned piece taking a critical look at some aspect of the literary world in Ireland, Britain or the United States. Each issue also contains a portfolio of work from a leading photographer.

IRISH PAGES is a non-partisan, non-sectarian, culturally ecumenical, and wholly independent journal. It endorses no political outlook or cultural tradition, and has no editorial position on the constitutional question.

The sole criteria for inclusion in the journal are the distinction of the writing and the integrity of the individual voice. Equal editorial attention will be given to established, emergent and new writers. IRISH PAGES does not associate itself with any prize, award, competition, "best-of" ranking selection, fundraising initiative, or other literary promotion that vitiates against the independence of taste and judgment.

Stepping Stones Across a Bog, Connemara
by Rachel Giese Brown
from The Earth Issue

"I enclose a check for another year's two issues, as your publication is a fantastic find. Even bought a subscription for my friend Elizabeth … I remember Belfast fondly and it makes a warm remembrance in a cold Vermont winter."

Jack Meyer
Subscriber, Vermont

SUBSCRIBE NOW

£16stg/€26/$34 *(for one year)* £24/€39/$46 *(for two years)*

(For postage outside Ireland and Britain, add £4/€6/$8 per year for Europe or £6/€9/$12 for the rest of the world)

Name ______________________________

Address ______________________________

____

Country ______________ Postcode ______________

Email ______________________________

Send as gift (*with card from* ______________) to above address.

Enclosed is my cheque/money order to IRISH PAGES for the amount of ______

Please charge my ◯ Visa ◯ Mastercard

Card Number | | | | | | | | | | | | | | | |

Expiry date ______________ Signature ______________

Subscribe now by posting this form to:

IRISH PAGES, The Linen Hall Library, 17 Donegall Square North, Belfast BT1 5GB
Email: irishpages@yahoo.co.uk Tel: ++44 (0) 2890 434800
or visit our website at www.irishpages.org

PRAISE FOR IRISH PAGES

"A wonderful achievement." *Michael Longley* Poet, Belfast. "IRISH PAGES is an important event in the history of Northern Ireland." *Rev Hilary Wakeman* Author, West Cork. "One of the finest journals I have seen produced anywhere in these islands in many years." *Gerald Dawe* Poet, Director of the Oscar Wilde Centre for Irish Writing, Trinity College Dublin. "A major development in Irish literature." *John F. Deane* Poet, novelist and editor, Dublin. "The most important cultural journal in Ireland at the present moment." *Jonathan Allison* Scholar and critic, Director of the Yeats Summer School. "Intensely non-provincial, the magazine accomodates the global and the avant-garde alongside the local and traditional ... The mixture is exhilarating ... THE BELL makes a doughty precursor for IRISH PAGES, which, in a similar vein, goes all out for sober excellence and inspired audacity." *Patricia Craig* Biographer and critic, *Times Literary Supplement*. "IRISH PAGES represents a new maturity in the life of the Irish periodical." *Belinda McKeon* Critic and journalist, *The Irish Times*. "IRISH PAGES' critical reception has been outstanding, especially gaining plaudits for its blending of local and global perspectives. The Editors see the magazine operating along the crucial intellectual intersections of the literary, the historical, the ethical and the social." *Malcolm Ballin* Literary scholar, Wales. "Because it seems to me they have created something of a new paradigm here – a literary journal that acts locally but thinks and reads globally. That's just what's needed, this deliberate, self-conscious and nourishing ecology of art, responsive to weather patterns worldwide while knowing when to open its umbrella. The editorial philosophy animating IRISH PAGES asserts that wisdom lies in looking not only inward, but also around, behind and over our shoulders: to see both ourselves and our place in a larger whole ..." *Askold Melnyczuk* Novelist, founding editor of *Agni*, Boston. "The new issue of IRISH PAGES is superb. It is hard to think of a journal in the British Isles today that can match its unflinching seriousness and elegance." *Iain Galbraith* Poet and translator, Germany. "I'm writing, really, to express my admiration for the quality of what you're publishing ... I admire IRISH PAGES hugely..." *William Trevor* Novelist, Devon. "IRISH PAGES is wonderful ..." *Susan Sontag* Essayist and novelist, New York City.

IRISH PAGES is a Belfast journal combining Irish, European and international perspectives. It seeks to create a novel literary space in the North adequate to the unfolding cultural potential of the new political dispensation. The magazine is cognizant of the need to reflect in its pages the various meshed levels of human relations: the regional (Ulster), the national (Britain and Ireland), the continental (the whole of Europe), and the global.

AMONG OUR CONTRIBUTORS

Chris Agee / Gary Allen / Neal Ascherson / Eileen Battersby / John Berger / Sven Birkerts / Wendell Berry / John Burnside / Rachel Giese Brown / Angus Calder / Moya Cannon / Ciaran Carson / Harry Clifton / Michael Coady / Patricia Craig / Andrew Crumey / Gerald Dawe / Michael Davitt / John F. Deane / Greg Delanty / Michael Donhauser / David Edgar / Hans Magnus Enzensberger / Leontia Flynn / Brian Friel / Sam Gardiner / John Gray / Eamon Grennan / David Grossman / Michael Hamburger / Hugo Hamilton / Francis Harvey / Seamus Heaney / Kathleen Jamie / Esther Jansma / Francis Jones / Julia Kristeva / Helen Lewis / Michael Longley / Seán Lysaght / Tom Mac Intyre / Deirdre Madden / Sarah Maguire / Fred Marchant / Enda McDonagh / Medbh McGuckian / Askold Melnyczuk / Samuel Menashe / Maire Mhac an tSaoi / Immanuel Mifsud / John Minihan / Zakaria Mohammed Alfonso Monreal / John Montague / Paul Muldoon / Mira Nair / Nuala Ní Dhomhnaill / Micheál Ó Conghaile / Bernard O'Donoghue / Liam Ó Muirthile / Cathal Ó Searcaigh / Louis de Paor / Glenn Patterson / Tom Paulin Sir Martin Rees / Tim Robinson / Gabriel Rosenstock / Raoul Schrott / Paul Seawright / W.G. Sebald / Brendan Simms / Peter Sirr / Gerard Smyth / Gary Snyder / Susan Sontag / Richard Tillinghast / Alan Titley / William Trevor / Daniel Tobin / Michael Viney / Casey Walker / Hans van de Waarsenburg / Bruce Weigl / David Wheatley / Charles Wright

and many others ...

BACK ISSUES

Inaugural Issue: Belfast in Europe (Vol 1, No 1)
The Justice Issue (Vol 1, No 2) *Empire* (Vol 2, No 1) *The Earth Issue* (Vol 2, No 2)
The Literary World (Vol 3, No 1) *The Home Place* (Vol 3, No 2) *The Media* (Vol 4, No 1)
The Sea (Vol 4, No 2)

witness, will not pronounce in the decorum of subject-verb-object sentence-structure during her contractions but will cry out in aspirates and plosives, in Aahhs and Oohhs, in Alphas and Omegas. And when the glistening child wails in its novelty, terrified by the blinding brightness of its own voice, her lips will be flaked and chalky from biting and bearing down.

But I'm not able to speak. I cannot tell the story. My mouth is all dental filling and no mercury. Ruins and scaffolding crowd it, the crater of a bad wisdom tooth and the dressings like tampons.

–Uhhh, I try to tell him. Uhhh.

–Ssshh, I say to the child in my arms. Ssshh.

Spiders are grooming their webs at the hall door. Snails haul themselves in hydraulic exhaustion up the glacier of the window in the wall. They are tears travelling back to where they started, a film run in reverse; and, as we go into the house, the set is still on. The news has come round again, on the hour every hour, and there's the rapist under the raincoat climbing into the police van. Flashbulbs rear around him like clubs and cleavers. I know nothing of his dark night. I stand in the broad daylight of my own existence, and other troubles, tragedies out there, are the tidbits of my recreation, the drink before dinner. So too the kid with the Kalashnikov in the dustbowl of some proxy state. He will be dead and buried before his photograph wins prizes in the actuality section of a Media Awards banquet.

–Ssshh, I say. Ssshh. It's all sibilants and labials: abba, baba, babytalk.

It is only when the babysitter stares at us that I realise my shirt is stained, soaked in fact, dipped in blood like a batik tank top, a map of Europe the wrong way up; and I'm embarrassed by this view of it, this vulgarisation of a child's coming of age, this affront to the subtlety of what has happened to her, of what she has happened upon in the day's befalling.

–Home again, home, she says. She says it in a drone from the thorax like someone who's gone upriver from the Jordan to the Ganges to intone the mystical phoneme *Om*.

Now it's the small hours, now it's two in the morning, the time the heart finds hardest. Cardiac ambulances roam the dual carriageway, their sweet soprano sirens a beachcomber's calypso. In the gloom of my child's bedroom the shapes of stuffed animals loom larger, their button eyes unblinking, their lips hanging by threads. For this is where I'm catnapping between shifts, with my glasses on and my shoes off, while my daughter crouches like a foetus in the bed where her journey began, and where my wife is shoring up her teeth in their flimsy sockets with the fingers of two hands propping the pulpy gums.

The rooms of children are my stepping stones, my stumbling blocks. That bedroom in West Belfast where I stayed as a graduate student was the habitat of a thirteen-year-old child. Rotors of a gunboat in the sky above her or the warning bin-lids of the backstreets could not deter her from filling a wallchart, from fulfilling it, with the dates of anniversaries, the details of appointments, and a series of Flo-pen P's she had illuminated like Celtic capitals in the column of every fourth week as she proclaimed Martha's Magnificat, the flow of her life, the decency of her bloodletting, from the heart of the Paschal mystery. And the kindergarten classroom of Palo Alto had its wallposters too, the pink elephants of Disney's Dumbo cartwheeling around the minyan at the AA meeting where a varsity lush who could lecture to a baseball stadium without a microphone opened his mouth and whispered praise of those who had stood by him until he dragged them down. Eighteen stone, he sits on his hands on a bansai bentwood chair with a toddler's Christian name on the back of it; and living water tumbles out of his eyes. The chalice he has shared is vinegar. Perhaps its fragrance is hyssop. He is as close to God as a man can be; he is as close to man as God can come.

There are books among the bears in this child's bedroom. When she was little, I read to her at night from Puss in Boots or Jonah and the Whale, doing the voices in the topsy-turvy of a try-out ideology, God in the domestic register of a mother's tones rather than boardroom bullypulpit, villains in the haughty falsetto of the heartless high meritocracy instead of the cackling of yokels; but of course it didn't work. We were each of us as confused as the other. So I returned the Lord to his prestige public school accent and I Am Who Am never said "It's me" again. Bullhorn and Begum were as inseparable as rant and rave.

Yet she would still kiss the Ladybird book when we'd finished reading it, kiss it and hold it up. That was because she'd seen the priest doing the very same at Mass, kiss the reading and lift the lectionary for the greeting of the Gospel in song. She knew that a book is precious, that a story is priceless, that we gather in the church to tell the stories that the storyteller told, and to tell as well the story of what happened to the storyteller and what happened because of him. As the parish benches creak like the deck of a ship, we sit in the nave of a vessel designed for soundwaves, for the slow unfolding of language, and the boat draws away from the lakeshore, from the shoreline where all life begins, and the storyteller is standing in the thwarts, watching the crowds who watch him, who await him, the word of life, the liveliness of his words, and now he can speak to them, subtly, straightforwardly, across the marvellous acoustic of water, the face of the deep, so that everyone can hear without the delay of the routine relays, without the stewards in each tenth row reporting self-importantly back to the stewards behind them.

-Lord, open our lips

-And we shall praise your name.

If Oedipus were a figure in scripture, in Kings or Chronicles, he wouldn't have savaged his eyeballs; he would have cut off his tongue or been struck dumb. By the same rule of reversal, Zechariah would have lost his sight but not the power of speech. Myopia and aphasia, blindness of the seer and muteness of the prophet, are the emblematic options of Athens and Jerusalem when those two cultures, our mentors and tormentors, seek to imagine our closeness, our closedness, our disclosed selves. True enough, it works the other way round too, as it must in such proximate geographies. Darkness is endemic in the Hebrew Bible and the Christian New Testament: from Isaac to Saul, from Samson to the pool of Siloam; on the other hand, the Greeks delight as abundantly in their bright, prehensile speech-acts and they explore as intensely the vulnerabilities of utterance – Orpheus and Cassandra – as any Hebrew for whom language, the sum of listening and hearing, praising and proclaiming, is the green rendezvous of the dialogue between God and God's people in silence and stillness. Yet Job's penultimate outcry – "I had heard of you by the hearing of the ear, but now my eye sees you" – is not the last word in the aniconic, auditory tradition. The transformation of Saul into Paul, his metonym and metanoia, dramatises the road to Damascus as the fork and flashpoint between two cultures: "The men who were travelling with him stood speechless, hearing the voice but seeing no one. Saul arose from the ground; and when his eyes were opened, he could see nothing". The fellow-travellers are struck dumb because they cannot see, because they cannot focus the experience in their sights. Their Greek idolatry of cognition makes recognition impossible; they subsist accordingly in the specular and the speculative enlightenment in which all vision ends up as double vision and in which the supernatural dwells in diminished form as the paranormal realm. But Paul arises. Because he has encountered the holy and the wounded of God in a meeting that is represented as aural, as the transitive intimacy of risk and response in the mucus membrane of language, he is blessed: he has heard and not seen; or, better, he has heard because he has not seen. For seeing, after all, is only verification; hearing is verity. Along the road to Damascus there is a crossroads; it is the road to the cross or from it. The cyclops eye of the encyclopaedia cannot decipher this intersection, this X which marks the spot. Paul, passing here hot-foot in pursuit of the Jesus of history, will discover in the red shambles of his own ambition the risen Christ of faith.

Isn't the Greek for "I know" also the Greek for "I have seen"? To see, to survey, to comprehend, to totalise: such is the imperium of the eye, inquisitive, acquisitive, the self as sovereign, a panoptic demigod gazing from a height on the horizontal bounty which his vision penetrates and impregnates. This is the Hellenic aim, the Hellenistic agenda; and Aristotle's classificatory travails, his retinal tirelessness, is in ways the hospitable analogue of Alexander's campaign to appropriate the territories of the earth, to enrol the whole world in a census, to survey Creation from the atrium of the male household. And it is an enticing prospect. It enticed Philo, a contemporary of Jesus, to fantasise about a version of the Law and the Prophets in which the acoustic physiology of the whole body of scripture would yield to a visual prosthesis, and we would see our nakedness instead of being told about it.

Yet I keep coming back to something more humble, more Hebraic, to the phatic and to the apophatic as well, not only to the sayings in scripture but to the saying of it, not only to its orations, speech or prayer, but to its orality. We make perhaps too much of the grandiose *ipse dixits* of Elohim which inaugurate the creation myths in the first book of Moses, for before the precedence of word over act, of mouth over hand, there is first the sound of the spirit moving over the face of the deep: there is breath, aspiration, possibility, pneuma. And this is personal, this is *per sona* – it brings into being not only Adam's exquisite bestowals of truly proper names on the eligible world around him, but also the first expression of the world engaged within him. In a maiden outpouring of tenderness and gratitude, the earliest recorded words of a human being in the Pentateuch celebrate the identity and distinctness of a partner. "This at last is bone of my bone and flesh of my flesh." Difference without division, reciprocity without doubleness: here is the echo-chamber of all dialogue.

In the hospital I said to her: Don't breathe a word. It isn't a figure of speech but a way of figuring all speech: as emanation, as exhalation, as spirit. And this is a Jewish mystery, not a gentile mystification. It goes beyond the verbal to the vocal. At two in the morning a parent can tell which of his three children is coughing under the covers in a bedroom above him; the frequency of a month-old baby's barely audible whine will wake a mother from a sleeping pill. An aged woman may watch a television documentary about her late husband's political accomplishments, but she'll watch it with the volume turned down; for the mantelpiece memories over the hearth are a manageable form of ancestor worship, sacral images over vestal flame, but the voice is the man, the word is the whole human presence proclaimed. Videos of the faithful departed standing in paper crowns at their birthday cakes can be fast-forwarded or slowed to the snail's pace of one frame after another. But the drop-mail messages which monitor our phone calls and which preserve the breath of life in quiet pericopes – "I am unable to speak to you at present. If you would like to leave a message, I shall try to answer your call" – lie in our bottom drawers with the tufts of hair we clip from those who have gone before us. To listen to these audio-tapes is to enter an unbearable plenitude. Even their silences bespeak us, the nasal inhalations, the sputum in the respiratory tracts, the lip perforating moistly along a coldsore. And so my Filipino flatmate of fifteen years ago would spend his stipend on ringing Tondo, Manila, and be at ease with the stalled, slowcoach sentences of his grandfather, for the man's handicap was no slur on him. Chuckles and tuts sufficed. It was a mystical discourse. Their breath condensed on the Bell satellites in outer space and misted the face of the deep before it returned to earth at the international rate in the deep communion of two human beings, of two humans being.

No wonder the prophets bit their tongues. No wonder they held their breath. Hot coals and warm coaxing it took to beguile them into the work of witness, the witness of words. Civil liberties activists who champion freedom of speech are apt to invoke eighteenth-century avatars; and those stalwarts in turn fixated on Rome in republican times and on fifth-century city statesmen in Greece. Yet their forgotten founding fathers are as much the contradictory obstructionists who gave prophetic witness to the people of exile and exodus as are the Periclean intellectuals in the Stoa of Attalos; but the Hebrew countersignatories, with a stronger sense of medium than of media, held on to the risk and jeopardy of sacred eloquence, held close to utterance as the outer expression of an inner disturbance, held fast to heartwork and hard work under the sign of language, whereas in the Greek mainstream the movement is from globe to atlas, oratory to laboratory, in a breathtaking demonstration of the instrumental universe through the language of signs.

It is the difference between power and authority. For the opposite of power is not powerlessness. It is authority. The cry of Jesus on the cross is not fluent, but it is eloquent; which is to say, it has the authority of its own powerlessness. Because it is eloquent, its adequacy perturbs us; because it is not fluent, it bewilders the onlookers. He is not calling on Elijah as the Jerusalemite bourgeoisie believe. He is calling on Eli, the God of Abraham and of Isaac and of Jacob. But because his lips are bloated, because his tongue is swollen and dehydrated, because his mouth is full of bloodcrumbs and the acids of sick, but most of all because he speaks in a redneck hillbilly Galilean accent that is too aboriginal for the metropolis, the spectators assume that he's petitioning a prophet and not crying out to the Father for Christ's sake.

After the vocative, silence: a sigh's length; after the cry, the breath. Not a last breath but a lasting one, a breathing out of staleness and slaver and carbon dioxide that wouldn't mist a mirror in its meekness and weakness but which will become in the fullness of time a tremendous wind, a crosscurrent, a breath of fresh air, oxygenating the apostles in the asphyxsia of their closets, and resuscitating them, mouth to mouth and word for word, just as the God of the beginning blew into the lungs of his likeness, so that those whose teeth had chattered in the pain of panic-attacks could speak in public on the feast of Pentecost in an incarnational vernacular with a prepositional abundance – speak out, speak to, speak for, speak from, speak with – to a multicultural world.

It'll be bright soon. The birds are at it already. Their quick retaliatory phrases dazzle the hedges like the mirrors that prisoners flash from cell windows. The binmen will be here any minute. One of them's a beekeeper. By day he grooms our garbage. At night the hive swarms on his hands. His hands are priestly and introspective. He could preside among the cups and cruets, but he's baling black bags full of beer bottles and sanitary towels. Yet his hands are immaculate.

– Well? I say.

I look at my wife's fingers and see the weals on the palps where she's been pressing the teeth in.

– It's no use, she says. We should stop now. We should let her sleep.

The teeth are in the palm of her hand. They are ridiculous, really; like the rubbish that long-haired anthropologists offer to tribesmen in New Guinea in order to win their trust.

– I don't think she wants me to throw them away, my wife says. I don't think she wants you to throw your shirt in the washing machine. I don't know what she wants. She's just staring up at the ceiling as if it was the Sistine Chapel.

I live with strong women, strange women. There is an ancient cross in a potato field not too far from where I love and move and have my being, and on it is carved a great graffito of Brigid with a crozier. This is as it should be. Strong, strange women have told me time and again that the tomb is empty; and I have come to believe the words out of their mouth.

She shakes the teeth in her hand.

– It's like a throw of the dice, she says.

Sometimes I hear God as a foetus hears music, the notes of a Mozart concerto through the walled lagoon of the uterus. Once or twice I've heard him clearly, like the time my good godfather jammed an upended metal coathanger in the hole where an aerial had been broken off the bonnet of his Herald Triumph, and suddenly the cabin of the car filled with Beethoven's Ninth Symphony. Perhaps I will someday hear him like the voice of the Jewish cantor who sang the Shema at a whitewashed farmhouse gable in Poland where a firing-squad was machine-gunning the inhabitants of a shtetl, and the exterminators stopped and leaned on the overheated barrels and listened in the smell of toilets and ammunition to a sound that rose and fell, rose and fell, like the flash of a needle threading a rip in the fabric of the nightsky.

Afterwards they put him in a boat and floated him out into the middle of a river so that they could lie on the bank, these Catholic, nationalist, middle-class boys in battledress, and let their cigarettes burn down to pillars of ash on their wedding fingers as the sweet tenor of his prayer drifted over the water.

– Lord, open our lips

– And we shall praise your name.

Today as I go to work I shall try to imagine; I shall imagine trials. I shall imagine the child in the wheelchair among the sycamore seeds who told me once that tomorrow begins on the stroke of midnight and did I know that? I shall imagine a man waking to the smells of steel and urine in the isolation unit of a prison and a woman who hasn't closed her eyes all night in the enormous, abandoned orthopaedic double-bed where her husband cut his toe-nails on the duvet a morning ago, and I shall imagine a boy with bazookas who juggles grenades for the flak-jacketed prime-time presenters in a desert full of tyre-tracks, and a doctor with a stethoscope who can sleep now on his day-off, who can cling to the sleeping girlfriend beside him like a man who's been washed ashore finally, out of the saline tumult of things, a man who has finally found solid ground he can stand on, a strand with two sets of footprints and the sound of the sea getting fainter as you walk inland. Then I shall start to imagine what I have so far only seen, a child with a sea-urchin's mouth asleep on a cushion in the midst of all this perturbation, this green, painful life. For that is the prerogative of faith: it leaves everything to the imagination and nothing to chance.

Christ to the left of me. Christ to the right of me. I can name this world of the flyover and the footbridge as Adam named the animals. But that may be a first naming, proprietorial, appropriative, the colonisation of the alien. The Other does not exist to be subsumed into us as an adjective or an adjunct. It is instead the reverse, as everything tends to be in the Jewish-Christian Tao: otherness works its mystery of grace upon us in such a manner that ego is transformed into self in the paschal chrysalis. So the second naming is a renewed listening, God's Word at Pentecost as human dialogue in the charity and euphoria of a new Adamic inventory – Parthians, Medes, Elamites, all of us – that recreates apartheid as partnership, purity as completeness, distance and difference as the breathing spaces of the Spirit.

I get into the car and the chemical smell of the night before, its stress and distress, is still strong. Chambermaids can tell you the state of a relationship from the fragrance of a room. The car has an odour of quarrels, the sour taste of a waterbarrel. Spiders have spun two thumbprints across the wipers.

When I was small a man told me the truth. Of course he swore me to secrecy. On the sixth day, he said, God created the sixth sense and gave it to us as a donor organ so that we would be the first talking animal. He had already given us smell and taste and touch and sight and hearing, he said. But the sixth sense was different again: it was speech; and the bones of the story of speech are to be found in the basic anatomy of the throat and the mouth.

As I drive along the motorway, I think of sounds and silences, liquids and dentals, of morphemes in the warm cave of the mouth, roosting like bats in the Palaeolithic antiquity of our tongues, and flying blindly by radar through a universe that is always and everywhere ashram and abattoir. Within earshot of wherever I bow my head, before me, behind me, sentences are being spoken that have never been heard of before. On buses and commuter trains stories are being distributed like food. I want to proclaim it, the beauty of human lips, their imagery and likelihood, on this day that is extraordinary like any other, this week-day, this strong day, this day of the Lord.

In a house across the road, a child is learning to speak. She is saying something. Is she saying Dada? And her mother rings New Zealand so that they can hear it too. Dada. In another house across another road, on the ground floor of a nursing home, a stroke victim is making mouths. You would think he was attempting to lift apples with his teeth out of a bucket of water at Hallowe'en; and you would be right to think so. He is imagining the impossible. He is coming into his own. He is saying Thank you. And the chaplain sits a fraction of the host on the inflamed tongue, a tongue of fire, and thinks that in a Greek hospital the man would have said: Eucharist.

So I go to work, and I type in the five letters of my daughter's name as the password to my word-processor. The screen sings and lights up at the mere mention of her.

Home again, home again. When I lifted her into the house like a bride, that was what she said. I stood in the hall and I felt homesick. There was a burning sensation on the tip of my tongue.

Now I have my heart in my mouth. Now I am hanging on to dear life by the skin of my teeth.

SIX POEMS

In our blood-stream.

KYRIE FOR A COUNSELLOR

i.m. Cearbhall O Dálaigh

The acapella of wolves
Is what I recall, the long low
Solo of the orang utan
And the Greek Orthodox baritone
Of the bull elephant in his pen.
What keys can unlock them now?

It is two in the morning, so,
In the fierce middle of Dublin,
All my two children ago.
I am typing on an Underwood
Your note of resignation,
Your last wistful aria.

Recitative of flamingoes
Italicizes the darkness,
A rush of silver lances;
And the toothless MGM lion
Rattles the railings of his cage
Like the warm gusts in the Underground.

Without training, without Typex,
I type it out *ad nauseam*:
The same six wry sentences
On the big embossed stationery,
One Rothmans per revision
As if it were almost a poem,

A death-haiku, a love-cry,
A genealogical litany
Of the dáileach, the counsellor,
Cearbhall, the giver of torcs,
My Charlie Chaplin godfather,
A patrino, no padrone,

With his Pentecostal tongue –
Irish, French, High German,
Italian and Esperanto –
House-karl, *primus inter pares*.
In your kitchen in the small hours
Foxes drank from the cat's saucer.

Once at a public swimming pool
You undressed before me, disrobed
To the stencils of your socks
On your slender Achilles' heels.
I saw your beautiful nakedness:
The boy's wrists, the baby pubis.

And once in a Botticelli brochure,
Browsing for breasts and bottoms,
I found the Prisons' Maintenance Act
With your annotated account of one
Procedural supervised flogging
In the year of the dog and Yuri Gagarin

As if you were trying to tell me
That the Paraclete must come down
To cleanse the Augean stables
Of the criminal justice system
That you hated and held accountable
To our crucified, liminal Godman.

Such keening and lamentation
From the Zoological Gardens
Where you carried me on your shoulders
To watch the sea-lions caper
Who would change their shapes at midnight
To dowagers, debutantes, girls

And a Greek chorus of androgynes
In the Delphic silver of church-bells,
Stepping out of their pelts
As the paper spills from my carriage,
Streaked and ghastly and crumpled,
With the saline odour of howls.

SOUNDING THE NAMES

for Pádraig Daly

Let us lift up the 2003 Irish Telephone
Directory like the Gospel book at Mass!
Let the folk-group greet it in song!
Let the congregation acclaim it!

Turn it one luminous page at a time
Like the Book of Kells in the college library
From the helmeted child with Down's syndrome
Paddling her waterproof kayak on the cover

Like an aboriginal Firbolg in a log
Canoe, like a grunting Viking oarswoman,
A monk in his giddy coracle, a Norman flotilla,
A Huguenot dinghy at Coliemore harbour,

All the yawls, ketches, sloops and surfboards
Of our long ascent downstream to this delta
More far-fetched than any raft or hovercraft:
A bobbing, upside-down, Biblical ark

With a manifest of names like an altar-list
Of the living and their great grandchildren:
Adelugba, Adeniyi, Adeyemo,
Adkins, Adler, Adlington, Afe,

Advincula, Adye-Curran, Ahern,
Ahmed, Aiken, Alexander, Al Azaid,
Anon, Anonymous, Another!
The A to Z of it, the Alpha and Omega!

But not forgetting the dormitory transports,
Not forgetting my grand uncle open-mouthed
And bare-breasted for the male medical orderlies
With their spatulas and stethoscopes

At Ellis Island weeks before Wall Street flooded;
Not forgetting the unfathomable dead
In the closed caterpillar trucks at the dry dock
Whose Trojan cavalry has receded like white horses

To the albs and surplices of the dozy ocean,
To the choirstalls of the lost souls in our blood-stream,
To the salt taste of the lenses in our glasses
And the carte blanche of our last, cleansing Atlantis.

STRANDED

Hope and history don't rhyme.
They just alliterate
If you aspirate correctly,
Eliza Doolittle-style.
But the metre is a mantra
Like the billboards on the motorway,
Miles from my route at midnight
Between head-lights and cat's eyes
And the signage of two statelets.

The thoughts of it still tranquilize
Like the blind-spot of the monstrance
In the Church of the Blessed Sacrament
Where we pray for our daily bread
To be polyunsaturated;
And the slogans of ad campaigns
That flash on stand-alone screens
Give a taste of eternal life:
A secondaire in Sicily,
The good orgasm from Guinness,
Resentment and desire
The art of all our business,
The business of all our art.
History hoped for a bonus.
That Mass is over. Go in pieces
To love and serve a lasting chrysalis,
Defiled by our own virtues
And the purity of our vices,
Our cultural Pax Penicillin
All crisis and no Christ Jesus.

But the murderers in their gowns
Who cannibalised his body
In the black mass of atrocity,
The eucharist of the cockroach,
Wave their honorary doctorates
At an uptown photo-shoot –
Their capped and crowned teeth flossed
To gloss and to gloss over –
On their way to the Parliament
Where politicians stress
Peace and reconcilement
Who have walked out on their missus,
Leaving the femmes de ménage
For the femmes fatales' wet kisses,
The kitchen-sink for a pink oasis
That dissolves into the desert.

And the meek will inherit the earth
As they always do and have done,
The geological pay-dirt
Of a cemetery whose janitors
In an equal, ecumenist's land
Beyond lambeg drums and feiseanna
And the birdless columbarium –
And beyond the beyond of myself
With my Carmelite in one fist
And my bullet-points in the other –
Will be Muslims from Bangladesh
Who believe in the Virgin birth,
In the fruit that falls in her lap
And her steaming, stable placenta.

THE BERLIN WALL

I came home from hospital to find the Wall fallen.
It was two years later. Like that prisoner-of-war old Gerhart
Walking home from the Ukraine the year I was born
To his whiskered mother at the border, with a photograph
Of a smiling adolescent in her hatband,
My feet hummed from the metalled roads. You were much older.

Cream for your crow's feet on the dressing-table.
I walked our baby round and round in the searchlight
Of the television set. Men and women were scattering
The writing on the Wall, the beautiful spray-can frescoes.
Her drool on my shoulder glittered like epaulettes.
The earthen smell of her bum purified the temple.

When there was war between the parents, rare wildflowers
Flourished among those land-mines. Herons colonised
The one hundred metres between pillbox and bunker.
Ornithologists from all over climbed the watchtowers
With Army binoculars that had night-vision.
The two of us prayed in a ward without moving our faces.

Her weight on my shoulder felt like a small stroke.
Diapers stirred on the line. They were flags of truce.
Hands reached through concrete holes and chanced their arms.
I would have woken you. I had lost that freedom.
The tremor in my hands was not medication.
It was the psalm of my body. It was the future passing.

That was three in the morning. I danced with a vomiting infant
Like a scroll of the Torah. Her mother dreamed it upstairs
In a Zimovane vision, in the deep sleep of the just.
I thought of a schoolfriend's father whose incendiary bombs
Cremated the kindergartens, and who went back
Two years later in the same Lancaster with ton after ton of water.

DOING TIME

On my first day in prep school
In 1964 A.D.
A man in the college blazer,
A sixth year with blond sideburns,
Asks me to sign a petition
For release from an African prison
Of a person called Nelson Mandela.
"Have you the time?" he wants to know
And I show him my whistling Swiss watch
From my Holy Communion cash-flow
As the handbell rings for class.

I grow up, I go to university
Where, for the time being,
I study clockwork, chronology,
The arrow of time itself
That is life-giving and lethal,
And marvel at the Eternal.
I have, in fact, the time of my life:
Eschatological time,

Existential time,
Proust's time, Bergson's time,
Memory and amnesia,
Endurance and duration,
The womanly curve of Einstein's time,
And in no time at all,
The punctual girl with the hourglass pelvis
Under the clock in the library apse
Who has slipped off her espadrilles
To smoke a Gold Bond on the stroke of twelve
As a seminarian stands for the Angelus.

I spend ten swift years at three such
Slow, time-honoured institutions,
Each with its ivied campanile,
Each with its timeless chimes,
Until, in the fullness of time, I find
There is no more time to lose.
It's a job or the dole. I am interviewed.

On my first day on a convent school staff
In 1984 A.D.
A blond schoolgirl picks at my jacket
As the buzzer rings for classes
And she says to me:"Have you time, sir,
To sign a petition for a prisoner in jail,
An African called Nelson Mandela?"

THE FINAL SOLUTION

Delos, for three centuries
An Asian Minor marketplace
For slaves and the subhuman.
Millions had passed that way.
We did it in a day
From the gay island of Myconos
That we'd tired of temporarily,
All kaftans and rave vocals.

What I remember most
Were the lizards sidling swiftly
In tha theatre like a fingerprint
Where Euripides had played
To the Greek *Untersturmfuhrers*
Weighing breasts and testicles.
Their swish in the grass made you wet
Your disposable paper panties.

Barbados was the next.
It took a fluke of weather,
The sand going grey in the face
Under rainclouds and gusting
Sea-squalls to gather all
The holidaymakers together –
Their sun-block, their ghost bikinis! –
In the modest new museum

Where the nipple-to-nipple brand –
SPCK in reverse –
Was the eighteenth century logo
Of a London bible society
For promotion of Christian knowledge,
And where Thomas Thistlethwaite liked
To shit in his classical colonnade
For a slave of the stool to panhandle.

Auschwitz will be the same.
Our children will live to see it.
A golf-course architect mapping
The eighteenth hole at a bunker
Where the sand is burnt *homo sapiens*;
Or elderly naturists walking
On the tips of their toes through the pine-trees
With their shoes and socks in their hands.

A poet, novelist, playwright, essayist and short-story writer, Aidan Carl Mathews was born in 1956 and attended Trinity College, Dublin. His most recent collection of poetry is According to the Small Hours *(Cape, 1998). "The Skin of Our Teeth" is the first reflection in a new book,* Laments into Dances: Chronicles of Faith and Culture. *He works as a producer with Radio Telefís Éireann.*

WHEN THE STORIES FLED

Leslie Van Gelder

Under the glacier.

When the Stories Fled

This was the year when the stories fled.

For as long as I can remember, a story or five, have always inhabited a space within me. Whether they make it from mind to paper has never mattered. If I am most honest to the relationship, I should say that the stories themselves have created me as a façade so that they can continue to exist. What I do in my day to day world is irrelevant, provided the stories continue to have a place where they exist and in their own worlds can be complete. Writing is the somewhat uncomfortable process of bringing the inhabitants of one whole world fully formed as they are, to another, with a sort of honesty that removes me from the process. Any attempts at arch manipulation will be sorely punished.

The stories, living as they do, require a certain sort of geography to move from one space to the next. I think of this as a place or an environment, where the conditions must be right for that change of form to take place. My work is to create the conditions for the stories to flow and then to catch them in words as they tumble out.

At least, that's how it was before the tumor.

The facts of the story are fairly simple. My husband, Kevin, had been diagnosed with lung cancer four years before. He had never smoked. The tumor had grown at the site of an old pneumonia scar. We blamed it on all kinds of reasonable things like emotional stress, as it had been born in the last months of his previous marriage, claiming it as some sort of physical byproduct of living in a house where the air itself was toxic.

We had all the right things happen. The doctors caught it early. The surgery was quick but painful. For four months Kevin was weaker but in that time he had healing days when he struggled, and regular days when he was his old self. We lived through it, put it aside, and moved on. We never thought of ourselves as "cancer survivors". We thought we were beyond it.

If academics fear anything, I believe they fear the words "brain tumor" above all else. I know this from an informal study of having had to tell our friends and colleagues last spring, that Kevin had developed a brain tumor, a metastasis from the original lung tumor which expressed itself four years after the original. Many, most especially the Oxford folk, would unconsciously stroke their own heads when I spoke with them, as if reassuring themselves that their brains were still whole. Others found they had to look away from Kevin's hairless head and the thin scar running down the right side, as if the physical manifestation of someone in the throes of the "unthinkable" was an affront to proper society. By the time he was in a wheelchair we were effectively alone. The only thing the Oxford people wanted to know was how we had come to discover the tumor. They wanted an edge should the same symptoms ever emerge in their own perfectly formed brains. They did not want to see what it did to body and soul.

Truthfully, neither did we. On a March afternoon in the John Radcliffe Hospital, when the registrar returned from Kevin's scans with the verdict of "brain tumor" I didn't want to know either. I burst into tears, and the embarrassed registrar, after presenting us with the news, nervously fled the room. Apparently, one is not supposed to cry upon hearing this sort of news. The NHS does not cover such things and it would be helpful if madam could get a grip on herself. And so I did.

I did the only thing I have ever known how to do and I have done it unconsciously my whole life. In the face of enormous emotional challenge, I freeze over, like a river suddenly turned to ice. I can move, exist, live in the outside world, maintaining my job, relationships, and a sense of humor. But within, I am a river of ice that suspends in animation all of the feeling I had before so that I can continue to "do what needs doing" without being consumed by the emotions of the moment.

I suspect this proclivity towards glaciation is genetic. My father, whose emotional wiring I seem to have inherited, had a similar capacity for coping with emotional enormity. It was expressed in the philosophy that "things still needed doing" and that we always needed to work off the premise that there's a very good chance that no one will come to help when you really need it. Whether that was a cynical response, one that walled off others, or a wisdom built out of his own experiences, the belief that we are not to expect someone else to come along and take care of things while we sit in an emotional heap runs very deeply in my family's mythology.

The glacier happens to be how it's done.

It is an unconscious thing, although in later periods, as the months wore on, I resisted it. In fact, the glacier only works in the short term for surviving surgeries and getting through the first hurdles. It is a way of putting off emotions until they become fully disembodied from the event. Later, when the crisis has passed, I call the second phase the "loose board from the tornado" syndrome.

In the short term crisis, the glacier allows for putting away of feelings and just coping with the current challenges and circumstances by carrying on as usual. Later, when it's safe to relax again and mind and body unwind, I find I am often hit one day with what feels like a stray board from a tornado that had blown by months before. I know of others who describe similarly the feeling of a sudden breakdown, weeping unconnected to an event, or getting very ill. All of those responses are somehow probably tied to the capacity to suddenly melt a glacier that has held in suspension so many fears and hopes that when they come tumbling down again as springmelt, they knock you to your knees because you know it's now safe to do so.

Worse still, they are completely disembodied. An emotion tied to a circumstance has a physical shape to it and a connection. An emotion unleashed without its cause is a disembodied force and the shape of it, so far perhaps from its vessel, is a dangerous creature indeed, the sort of thing that one reads about in myth. Much of my story ahead is about just this sort of disembodied emotional Manitou.

The problem with the tumor was that it outlived the duration of the glacier and I was left in a world I had never inhabited before.

The short version of the story goes something like this. Kevin had the brain surgery in the first week in April, ten days after the original diagnosis. We spent those ten days in a whirlwind, getting our lives in order, relying on help from family, feeling suspended by not knowing what would come next but also grateful that there was action. There were mistakes on the part of the hospital at which we could rail, and fear that Kevin would wake up from the surgery and have no idea who I was. He came out of the surgery buoyant – his lost coordination restored, his sense of humor intact, and thanks to the steroids, full of a million ideas he wanted to act on right away.

It seemed we had survived the first storm. We waited for the radiation to start, and three weeks later he embarked on a course of daily radiation to his brain. We took the bus up each morning, dutifully waited with the other people whom we'd come to know from the small corner of Waiting Area 4, and then carried on with life. Kevin was tired from the radiation, but no worse than an afternoon nap and the need to just take care of his strength.

A month after the radiation ended, Kevin fell asleep. I can see him now, dressed in his orange shirt, his vest and jeans. He would wear those clothes for weeks to come as he was suddenly, inexplicably, unable to do anything more than sleep. In the brief times when he was awake, he told me of the cat walking around the room (we don't have a cat), the animals that had come alive from the shapes of knots in the closet woodwork, and a collection of disc and baguette shaped items that he felt he had to sort. He pulled into himself with the force of a collapsing star, and I found myself in the strange space-time continuum of trying to keep him in "this world" and stretching myself further and further from the "day to day" world which still depended on me to work and keep us afloat. For someone who has always been interested in the relationship between Place and Story, I found the space I inhabited as being more or less its antithesis. I existed in the world of time, but not a time I had ever known before since my interest in time has been either looking forward or looking back. Instead, we inhabited a place where time had no narrative. It was not an evolving story. It was simply a location.

The day was broken into units of "trying to feed Kevin" (who at this stage was reduced to eating one weetabix a day and only if I begged) and trying to keep up with my work as there was nothing else because I could not look to any future and by not looking to any future, I was effectively cutting myself off from my imagination so as to survive.

All I could do was inhabit an interminable present which was presenting, for at least four months, what looked like a downward trajectory. Kevin grew inexplicably weaker; the doctors started him on chemotherapy anyway and six weeks later I brought home a wheelchair in the hopes of being able to at least get Kevin out of the house. For seven weeks he slept and slept and slept. When he woke again he was the shadow of the man I knew.

He had lost nearly 50 pounds, he could barely connect his thoughts, he couldn't walk down the stairs, and his world which had been so large was reduced to thin strands which needed constant feeding of hopefulness and positive belief. For him, I would lie. I had to.

No matter what I felt inside, I swallowed my own responses to make sure he heard what he needed to hear. I am no saint and I made mistakes, but my goal was to keep him from feeling more pain than he needed. If I cooked him breakfast at his request, and he took one bite and said it was awful, I just threw it away. I didn't respond to the part of me which screamed out at what a waste of time and energy that had been. If he wanted to go up to town in the wheelchair, and we got there for five minutes and he wanted to go home, that's what we did. My belief was that he needed to be able to try things out without any emotional punishment for the experiments that didn't work. Otherwise, he would feel guilt on top of already feeling, almost twenty four hours a day, like he wanted to throw up. The physical geography of a collapsing star has a gravitational pull like none other. By nature, he was pulled downward and by sheer will, I was trying to pull us upwards again.

I paid the price for my willingness to put my normal reactions aside in three ways. The first, which began on the day the words "brain tumor" entered our world, was that I stopped sleeping. It was as if there were a finite amount of sleep that our bed could contain. If Kevin were going to sleep 23 hours a day, then I would sleep the other one, but not much more than that. I came to inhabit 2 and 3 a.m. Got to know the night stars, the shape of the river shimmering on the ceiling illuminated by the yellow street light across the way. This lack of sleep still plagues me. I think of it as an erratic left by the glacier, somehow blocking the valley to sleep. Eventually, it, too, will get worn away.

The second came towards the middle of July, while we were still in the midst of the long sleep. Earlier I said that when I have inhabited a glacier, it has almost always been for a short term. I have not necessarily had many experiences of very long-term challenge and I have always doubted my own sense of stamina. In the midst of the rainiest summer in English history, I remember the moment of looking into the bathroom mirror and not recognizing myself. I looked at someone I didn't know.

Kevin would often look at me and say I looked so tired, which I'm sure I did. This was something else. I felt I had lost the edges of my body almost completely. My inner sense of who I am was still powerfully present, in fact had been challenged so many times a day that I often wondered if I was starting to resemble a piece of molten steel, but the outer version of me had simply become an unknown.

I took measures to find my edges. I bought a pair of earrings that were heavy and helped me locate my head. I started wearing perfume on a daily basis, spraying it only on my hands so I could find them. I don't know if any of it really helped, but at least I felt I knew where my edges were.

When I look back now, I believe I know what happened. I was simultaneously trying to inhabit multiple worlds. In the "first world" the one where my work lives and the bills need paying, time moves along at a fairly well agreed upon speed. Send an email, get a response. Need groceries, go shopping. That world had an ever-present future unfurling at a relatively expected rate of 28 days to pay the bills and 48 hours on emails, with all points somewhere in between.

In the "second world" I inhabited with Kevin, it moved only moment to moment and was defined and bound by the degree of the pain he was experiencing. Pain is without time. The only time it has is "now" and "over." As other cancer survivors have described, when you're in these periods, especially the period of chemo, there are no plans because everything is a variable. Instead of having time, I would say that you have weather. And at any given moment, a storm can break, even under what appear to be sunny skies. There is no making of concrete plans. You cannot look ahead. Instead, you live moment to moment and have to be in a constant state of readiness with the willingness to adapt to whatever the circumstances create.

Readiness breeds one set of senses, "future-looking" breeds another. The two do not co-exist well as one requires a certain faith in variables and the other is a willingness to adjust immediately to a sudden change, so it is more of a continual environmental scan than anything long-range.

The "third world" was the one in which I swallowed my own responses to situations for the sake of Kevin's bigger picture. This meant two things. With him, naturally, it meant me putting aside my own reactions to give him a better outlook. The challenge for me was that he is not only my husband, but my best friend, and as he disappeared into himself, I could not talk with him about how I felt.

My fears, my thoughts, my understanding of what was happening to and with him could not be processed because he was the person with whom I had always done that, and yet because of the circumstances there was no way to share those thoughts and feelings with him. I was effectively alone in the most frightening place I had ever been with no place to express those feelings and no one with whom to process them.

In retrospect, that was my choice. I have friends who would have and who did listen. But they weren't in the midst of the space we inhabited; and the power of the gravitational pull of Kevin's illness, my need to keep working, and all points in between, seem to have effectively torn me apart.

The end result was that in this time period, I lost the capacity to recognize myself in a mirror.

And the stories fled.

I knew there had to be a sacrifice and I knew that the sacrifice had to be that which I valued above all other things. By dividing up my voice, swallowing my responses for the sake of Kevin, becoming someone fierce when I took him out in the wheelchair, I lost access to the place where the stories used to come to me.

At first, I could hear the characters all still there. In fact, at times, I felt they pressed up against me, annoyed that I was neglecting their egress. I saw aspects of stories I had never considered before and felt a sort of creative intensity, most especially from a story set in France which I had hoped to finish this year. The main character in it feels an intense loneliness and outsiderness, and I think that feeling of not fitting into any world made his story come to me all the more vividly.

But try as I might, when I went to write, the well began to run dry. First I wrote in spite of it, and then I found a lethargy that would come in the moment I went from mind to pen. I might be able to get a paragraph, sometimes only a few sentences, and finally just the thought of the writing made me tired.

The willing separation of my voice from my circumstances, the months of sleeplessness, and the fear of futures which bound me to living only in the moment in perpetual circumstantial readiness, seems to have sealed the door between the stories and myself. I believe they are still there, in fact I know they are. But their absence is some part of some sacrifice that I had to make. I remember reading about people who sun-dance and those who do saying that the bones they attach through their chests from which they drag buffalo skulls until they have worked their way through the skin, are usually not the sacrifice itself. Those cuts are just a guarantee – some outward scar – for what has gone on deep inside.

If I learned anything from this year, I learned that I am a writer. I knew it before, but to lose something so valuable is always the best way to go from knowing to believing. I know it not from any form of skill, but because I was confronted with the moment of sacrifice. When I had to give up something to save someone I love so intensely, it was the only thing I really had that felt of any value to the world. I gave it up without realizing it in part because I was utterly unwilling to give up on Kevin. He is here today and he is getting better. That is enough.

For six months now I have had an empty space where the stories were. It is the strangest absence, like being in a house where you only occasionally hear the scurrying of mice in the attic to remind you that something is there. I have turned to my camera, the place where I have gone when I need to think without thinking. If I am to find the stories again, I imagine it will be along the path where I lost them. I need to write my way back into the place from once they flowed.

I read *Little, Big* in the midst of this drought and I have Patrick Curry to thank for it, because there is much to be said of that world of enchantment, its complete worlds within worlds, and the ways of being patient enough to bring some form of trust back to communicate with those folk on the other side. I had been warned at the outset of the journey Kevin and I took, that there would be dark woods. That warning was a true one and some of the places I've been I would be happy to leave off the map for future travelers. To be free to venture safely in the land of imagination in part requires this world to have some safety to it. Without one, the other withers.

While Kevin has a scar on his head to show what he's been through, I have nothing visible; just an absence to show what I have lost, but neither of us feels that we are fully healed.

For now, I have no stories to share that are of the variety I like, but in the pages that follow are the threads of stories slowly coming back to life. They whisper now, but in time, I hope they will say something worth hearing.

Carving

poses a question of opposites. We come to believe that in life our goal is to add to, to enhance, make more so instead of less. And yet, in the carving of a thing we remove, take away, shape and reveal an essence that may have been hidden beneath; or have to confess to the myriad possibilities which any one stroke of the blade creates.

Kevin's surgeon wore a bow tie. I have no recollection of his face, only of looking as closely as was polite at his hands. In the evening before the surgery he wrote his initials on Kevin's neck and drew an arrow pointing to the place where the lasers would peel away his skin, making him look like a "this end up" box.

After the surgery, I asked the surgeon how it had gone. He was back in his bow tie. "In the bucket", he replied blithely. I had to ask, did that mean he had gotten it all or that we were in for a hard time. "It's in the bin," he answered, "all of it."

Months later, at high table, we met a colleague of the surgeon's. "Who did your scar?" as if it had been a new pair of perkier breasts or a paint job for the house. With some trouble, we eventually produced the surgeon's double-barreled name.

"Ah yes, capital fellow! Did he tell you he was one of the great Oxford rowers in his day?" the robed don asked with his eyes lighting up. I mentioned that it hadn't come up in our conversation about the removal of Kevin's brain tumor. "It was a thing of beauty to see him row," the fellow answered, looking away from Kevin's pure white scar, "a thing of beauty."

A Number

Every time we arrived at the hospital we were quizzed on Kevin's NHS number, his address, his date of birth. His numbers were woven into a plastic band he wore on his arm. The first thing we did each time we came home was cut off the band. It was small, plastic, and symbolic of a shackle. Kevin would look at his hands and arms, counting the number of holes from the bloodlettings and poisonings.

When he disappeared into his dreamspace he came out of it through a pathway of numbers. He lost the names for parts of his body. Instead, they became numbers and geometric shapes. His feet were number 3. His mouth was the shape of a long baguette. Each number became a color, and each color held a shape. By holding on to those colored pieces of the world like a rope ladder, Kevin climbed back out of the dream space and into this world again.

Seeds

The air was still full with the smell of lilac when my step daughter, Miriam, and I boarded the red number 15 bus from the Radcliffe Hospital. We had been with Kevin all day before leaving him for surgery in the morning.

Between us was the whole collection of things we couldn't, maybe didn't want to say, about what the next day would bring.

"So, there's something I've been meaning to tell you." Miriam leaned her tied head against the window. "Nick and I are going to start on a family this year."

By the time we were off the bus, walking down St. Aldates in the dark, we were on to the politics of six grandparents, the thought of raising children in London, and a very bright future.

Miriam's conversation that night was one of the greatest gifts I've ever had. I don't know if she was even aware of the connection between the possibility of her father's death and the need to talk about having children. But, I knew.

As Kevin went into surgery the next morning I held for him an image of a grandson sitting on his grandfather's knee, reading very intently, *If a Tiger Comes to Tea*.

By autumn, after the worst of summer, there was a seed, and then a story, and then a secret, and then just a little over a year after that night on the bus, a little boy – the first of the April children in this antipodean family ever to be born in spring.

Unicorns

There are few rare sounds in the world – I think of them as aural unicorns – the sort of thing you might glimpse once or twice in a dark wood or cherish for its rarity. One is the sound of the one day in autumn when leaves fall and land upon other leaves rather than falling all the way to the ground. There is such an intimacy to that sound – the softness of fallen leaf on still-attached leaf – like caressing the cheek of the wind.

The other sound is 3 a.m. snow - before the ploughs have been called while the sun is still falling, illuminated in the triangle of street light. Hush snow, the softness of the air. The kind of sound and soundlessness the penitent monk craves.

There is a third sound I know now, but unlike the other two, it is one I hope never to hear again. The sound of Kevin's snow-white hair falling to the ground around him like an inner snow. Every time he ran his fingers through his hair on that rainy May Sunday, another drift. A tiny ripping sound, like a cloud pulling away from a star as drifts piled in the corners behind his chair.

The sound of hair snowing on a rainy Sunday afternoon. Snow falling, that beautiful sound. Hair falling, leaves in the wind, the dead briefly resting in the arms of the living until a wind pulls them both down.

And then my beloved's singular spring snow.

By late afternoon I could see a pink scalp. Aging by the minute, Kevin finally looked up sadly and said, "Please shave it".

Kevin sat in the kitchen in his orange robe, handing me the razor. "It's ok, do it", he said as I ran my fingers through his soft white hair. I had always called it polar bear fur for being so hollow, light and white.

I cried. Kevin couldn't see me as I ran the razor over his head.

Later, I would cry the first time I pushed him in the wheelchair, the first time he was hooked up to the chemotherapy, the day when he told me about the cat in the bedroom, and the day he told me 4:15 was pink and that the time in which we were living was 168 and that his feet were number 3.

Those were all tears Kevin never saw. There is a sound perhaps of tears that fall behind someone so that they might never see them lest they hurt someone in pain all the more. They, like my 3 a.m. snow, are muffled by the air around them so as not to fill a space. They should be a raging waterfall or a howl from some primordial place, but instead it becomes a silence of chasms, of wind sucked inward, of the quiet of space of just ordinary tears falling because your beautiful husband is bravely facing losing his hair. Rather than hear that sound of leaf loosing itself from the branch or the hair pulling itself from the scalp, he had asked you to cut it all away.

When it's over he runs his hand across the smooth space we will come to know for the next seven months.

His hair made no sound upon its return.

Or perhaps my ears were not well attuned enough to know the sound of fresh green grass pushing up through the earth on the first spring day.

The Bodied – and the Disembodied

I had not intended to focus so much on bodies, but it seems I have been questioning the idea of whole and full versus broken for some time now. I am drawn to hands, perhaps because of the work we do in the caves, but perhaps because they speak of who we are, and to feet, where we have been.

I own a sculpture in the African style of a blind drummer who lived and played in Tanzania in the 1980s. He was inspiring enough to be the subject of many sculptures and paintings in his time.

I don't recall when the sculpture was broken and repaired at the neck, but it seems to me he wears a face which defies being defeated by something so simple. Instead, the scar seems to suit him and he plays on.

When Dina Rabinovitch Died

I cried more than perhaps I should have for someone I had never met. We were at the Jericho Café, recaffinating after another of Kevin's check-ups. This morning he was without the wheelchair and only with a walking stick. It seemed a morning to celebrate.

I had been away for a few days so when I picked up the paper to see Rabinovitch's obituary, I was blindsided. Tears came from nowhere. I hadn't known her at all and yet I felt I had lost a rare friend.

Rabinovitch was a reporter for *The Guardian*. She had developed breast cancer during the same period when Kevin had his first tumor. The Guardian, seizing the marketable opportunity, gave her a regular *G2* column called "The Enemy Within".

For four years I followed her story. She was honest and forthright, telling stories of how her family were or were not coping with her cancer. Her young son Elon regularly featured as Rabinovitch was both amused and taken with his regular commentary about her absence or presence of breasts.

In one of her last columns, she wrote about turning down an offer to be on BBC television because she couldn't be sure, from hour to hour much less minute to minute, whether or not she would be well enough to participate. I knew what she meant. How many small opportunities we had declined for simply not knowing whether or not there would be a pool of energy much less a steady stomach on any given day. I suddenly found her to be a rare companion in this journey. This was in early October.

By November she was dead.

The thing with Dina Rabinovitch was that I was sure she wouldn't die. She had a column in the newspaper. She looked good in the picture. In her last few columns she had even dropped the typically blasé voice of *The Guardian* reporter and had told stories about how it really was for her. I was sure this was a sign of journalistic evolution. It didn't seem possible that the media would let her die.

But she did.

I remembered the article she had written when she was first trying to get her book published. She told the stories of the editors and agents who told her that "Cancer memoirs are so overdone" and that "no one was interested in another cancer story. Did I have anything else?"

That prohibition about writing about the cancer stuck with me and I, too, thought this is something about which I shouldn't write. When people asked, I tried not to tell much detail. In Oxford, that was easy as people really wanted things to be "back to normal" and no one wanted to know. Friends further away did want to know the details. It was a relief to talk or write about them. Ill health seems relegated to some shameful status, as if by knowing the details one is subject to the contagion.

After Dina Rabinovitch, I decided that at some point I would write about what we learned along the way. The more I met people who told us to "just put it behind us" the more I thought of Dina Rabinovitch who would never have let it rest. But now when I think on her, on this, I hope that she may at last rest in peace.

What We Pray For...

Kevin hated hearing that someone was praying for him. His years of studying science/religion had perhaps made the subject even sorer since he knew how much research money had been thrown towards the question of whether or not praying for someone actually had a positive effect.

In March, just around the time the tumor was found, an article ran in one of the science journals showing that not only did prayer not work, but that many people were negatively affected by the prayers. I have no idea how such things were measured.

Kevin used to lecture in his courses that people feel the need to have a sense of meaning and purpose but that they could just as well send their prayers to a paint can as to God if they believed in the power of the paint can. It is the belief, to the individual, which proves most important of all, not the actual outcomes.

I was sorely tempted to believe in a god who might be able to provide some meaning while we were adrift. When I looked for that God, I found the wind whistling through me, and a few dried and crusty old paint tins.

I seemed only to be able to believe in the swallows who flew over the Thames at dusk. They didn't promise me anything. They didn't deliver. They just looked so perfectly graceful arcing across in the soon-to-be night sky.

Three a.m.

I have great affection for 3 a.m. so much so that I believe in a certain 3 a.m.-ness, a quality of light and sound all its own. It is the time of snowfall, the world in a perfect hush, the time when the Pleiades come down and press their seven bright noses against panes of glass to see what night sleep might be.

At 3 a.m. the world is at its largest and most full of possibility simply because it is the time of dreams. To wake from that space and to walk into a wake-time does not seem to free us from the domed expanse of dreamspace around us.

Keats knew this time well. It was the time of the nightingale, the fabric of negative capability, that fine line between the free flow of imagination from some wellspring akin to dreaming and the manipulation of the path in the hope of finding what we might call enchantment again.

Not all 3 a.m.s are good. What is a grain-of-sand worry in daylight becomes monstrous in the darkness, roaming the edges of the bed multiplying in size, magnitude, and worry. Turning on the light will not make it flee. The faint glow of the computer in the corner may make it worse. The 3 a.m. demon, also bred of the same wellspring, can only disappear fully in the dust-mote light of morning. Sabers of light cutting through window panes can reduce the 3 a.m. demons to grains of sand. A grey day or the pound of morning rain can keep the demon alive, give it even greater shape and form, maybe even a place to live and a hot meal.

It is the other 3 a.m. I'd like to think about now. The one where the sound of the clock moving drives you out to walk barefoot into the night. Maybe there are stars in the canopy above. Maybe the clouds which only came in that night color, a glow like damsons lit from inside.

The 3 a.m. stars are different from the ones you know. Orion lies on his side. You imagine him leaning up on one elbow, stretched out in the grass, his long hair hanging off his shoulders, eyes glittering, while Sirius lies asleep in the sky-grass breathing heavily the way Labrador retrievers do when they're dreaming.

The quiet of 3 a.m. is the hush of expectation. It is the world emptied of one day and without the form of another. Mountains fade into sky for a rest, not yet needing to reform themselves into pre-dawn silhouettes. Time is at its fullest at this meniscus of the day when even the birds are quiet enough to make the world feel almost empty but for the non-sound of dreaming.

Navigation by Starlight

The great navigators of the Pacific built their star charts into the very bodies of their canoes and through the rise and fall of the night sky could locate themselves.

The stars were spirits of the dead. Not gone from this world – merely moved from motion on the ground to become earth-anchors above.

Honor

This is not a beautiful picture.
It is a yellow hammer's nest.
I scared the mother off her nest one summer's afternoon.
She never came back.
This is a photo of the nest she abandoned out of fear.
I have no photo of all of the things I abandoned out of fear.

How We Survived

I wonder that now. Now that we're on the other side of the pain. Now that the days seem to be the right number of hours. Now that time moves again instead of standing frozen in the middle of the glacier fearing for all the things that might be, could be, and are.

I did not find God. One rainy morning, five weeks into Kevin's Big Sleep, I stood outside the happy-clappy St. Aldates Anglican Church and considered whether or not someone would bring me a cup of tea or maybe a casserole if I threw myself on the mercy of the church. I figured it would be some sort of coup for them to get not only a new parishioner, but a conversion.

I will confess now that it was among my lowest moments.

Standing out in the rain, looking up at the church windows and contemplating whether or not I could fake any interest in Jesus for the sake of a cup of tea, I heard my mother's voice in the back of my head.

"You would throw away 5,000 years of Jewish history for someone to bring you a Tesco's frozen steak and kidney pie? You don't even like steak and kidney pie."

And so temptation passed.

My cousin in London told me later that I wouldn't have even gotten a re-heated cottage pie. "It's just not done here," she said prosaically, "It's nothing personal."

I have never felt as alone as I did in those summer months as Kevin spiraled downward. I am told that I became fierce. In September after a day carrying Kevin's wheelchair across Pompeii, I asked him what adjective he would use to describe me. He said, "Wolfish".

I didn't want to be a wolf. I didn't want to try to navigate the streets of Oxford with a wheelchair. I didn't want to hear from the osteopath that when she touched Kevin she thought he felt like he was filled with a thousand ships, all on fire.

I just wanted to go home.

Home was, is, a place on the other side of the world. There are mountains there whose names I don't know, but whose shape filled up the inside of me. When I had no strength, I found those mountains. They seemed to be there, quietly, constant, ever-present.

They had been beneath glaciers before.

They now had waterfalls running at their feet.

They taught me how to survive.

Now, I look forward to a future, as scarred and smoothed as the mountains I know,

stirring wild lupin in valleys
where glaciers once stood,
waiting for the stories who fled,
to slowly return.

In memory of Kevin

And with gratitude to Ron who said there's something essential in writing it down.

March 2008

Kevin Sharpe died, with his wife present, on 6 November 2008, in Dunedin, New Zealand.

Leslie Van Gelder was born in New York City in 1969 and took degrees in British and Native American literatures at, respectively, the University of Michigan and the College of New Jersey. She has published a collection of essays, Weaving a Way Home *(University of Michigan Press, 2008), as well as numerous articles on cave archaeology. She teaches at the Richard Riley College of Education, Walden University, and lives in the Rees Valley, New Zealand.*

THE MOURNERS

Francis Harvey

Over the loose sea-gravel.

"Isn't Hilda simply a marvel, so brisk and business-like, and not a tear so far?" Mary was speaking to one of the innumerable country cousins who had come to pay their last respects to her sister Hilda's husband, William John Lynam. She did not know her name. In fact, after 15 years of married life in Dublin, she hardly knew any of their names as, during the last few days, they stood or sat around the house in little awkward self-protective groups whispering like conspirators among themselves and watching the comings and goings of the town's middle-class citizens out of the corners of their eyes with a mixture of envy and admiration.

"Oh yes, yes indeed, she is, she is, she is", replied the country cousin quickly.

She was a middle-aged woman dressed in a black ankle-length coat and a tight black cap; she had hard worn hands and a red beaky face. Then she relapsed into silence, coughing nervously at times with exaggerated decorum into a crumpled flower-patterned handkerchief she clutched in her hand like a badge of mourning.

It was the morning of the funeral Mass and somehow, in the crowded drawing-room, Mary had found herself wedged in between this woman and the edge of the sofa. Everyone was waiting for the coffin containing the corpse – Hilda had insisted on keeping the body in the house until the day of the burial – to be borne downstairs to the hearse. The house was full of people gathered together in groups, sitting and standing, in the drawing-room, the sitting-room, the dining-room, the hall, the first and second landings.

There was a continuous subdued chatter all over the place. Now and then a face peered round the edge of the drawing-room door, looking for someone, and Mary would wonder whose that vaguely familiar face was: a friend or a relative she had not seen for years; a face that had coarsened or aged, become lined or fleshy, hair that had thinned or turned grey. At times she was devoured by an intense curiosity but she knew that it would be useless to ask the country cousin wedged in beside her. A feeling of irritation was slowly taking possession of her but she felt constrained to make another dutiful attempt to engage the country cousin in conversation.

"I do hope she continues to bear up like this, especially at the grave", said Mary.

"At the grave? Is she . . . is she actually going to the grave?" The country cousin's voice expressed shocked surprise.

"Yes", replied Mary matter-of-factly, "she is. Indeed, she insists."

"But", said the country cousin, "in these parts as a rule the women don't . . ." she broke off.

"I'm quite aware of *that*", replied Mary crushingly, in secret perversely pleased at the country cousin's reaction to the news that one of the local mourning customs was to be disregarded. "But there you are; you know the kind of a person my sister is: she just insists on going and there's nothing we can do about it." Mary, who was beginning to extract a sort of irrational compensatory revenge from the woman for her cornered situation, and who was maliciously amused at her attitude to this breach of traditional observance, decided to take matters further. "And that's not all", she added.

"Not all?" echoed the country cousin, avid with curiosity.

"No", replied Mary, "in fact, at the moment, I don't think the Canon and she see eye to eye at all and I'm afraid a nasty situation might develop." She paused.

"Nasty situation?" cut in the country cousin, open-mouthed.

"Yes indeed", replied Mary, "it's about these offerings, you know, and a thing like that might cause her to break down completely."

"Offerings?" said the country cousin, gaping at her for a moment. ". . . Well, I did hear something that William John, Lord gave mercy on him, left a tidy sum to the clergy instead of offerings, but . . ." She waited for Mary to go on.

"Yes", said Mary, whose husband invariably cultivated a harmless brand of anti-clericalism after three large whiskies and who herself liked to cut a dash as a very emancipated liberal, "as you say, William John left a large sum to the clergy of the parish in lieu of these offerings. And you know how, like all of us, he hated the whole awful business – taking money over the corpses of the dead. Ugh!" Mary grimaced with disgust. "But then there's something about a precedent being set that worries the dear Canon so much."

"Yes, yes . . . an awful thing . . . but do you really think there might be " – she paused, and with an effort brought out the word – "trouble?"

"You never know", replied Mary relentlessly, "some of these clergymen can be so arrogant. Anything might happen." She stopped to see the effect of her words.

"Oh, I hope not, I hope not. For your sister's sake, of course. It'd be terrible . . . terrible . . ." She paused, then went on brokenly. "You . . . you don't think . . . in the circumstances . . . that it might be better . . . better to have offerings?"

"*Have offerings* and go against my late brother-in-law's last wishes?" Mary simulated a tone of the utmost horror. "Why, that would be an appalling thing!"

"Of course, of course", the other woman broke in, hastily drawing back from the verge, "that would never do . . . never . . ."

"Certainly not", said Mary decisively, "Hilda would *never* go against her late husband's last wishes. And anyway, apart altogether from his will, he repeatedly told her when he was alive that there were to be no offerings at his funeral."

"You're quite right," said the country cousin, "quite right of course." She paused. "But couldn't . . . ?"

Mary never discovered what the country cousin was about to suggest because at that moment there was a series of heavy thuds from the room above their heads, where the corpse was being coffined, the sound of heavy footsteps and creaking floor-boards, and a powdering of lime-flakes fell from a small crack in the ceiling. At once a hush fell on the drawing-room and eyes were cast up reverently towards the room above. Some people made the sign of the cross. Then a wavelet of whispers rose and fell in the room, people nodded their heads solemnly and coughed discreetly, moved uneasily, and looked in the direction of the door. Outside one of the windows Mary saw the dark snout of the black glittering hearse nosing silently up to the door like a huge shark. She shivered.

The little groups in the drawing-room began to break up and there was a general movement toward the door. Mary excused herself and slipped out into the hall. It was thronged with people watching the four coffin-bearers – two brothers of the dead man and two employees from his factory – shouldering the heavy ornate coffin down the wide carpeted stairs and across the crowded hall to the hearse drawn up at the open door. In the back hall one of the elderly maids – for some reason Hilda did not like young female servants in the house – was sobbing audibly and the family solicitor hastily emerged from a back parlour wiping his lips with a handkerchief after a cup of tea. There were crumbs on his immaculate black waistcoat. Outside on the driveway cars were taking up position and groups of men stood about chatting. In the distance, down where the valley ended at the edge of the sea, slowly but clearly in the autumnal silence, a church bell began to toll for William John Lynam's last journey to the town in which he had prospered so well.

But Mary was watching Hilda. She had gone upstairs to have a last look at the corpse of her husband before they screwed the lid of the coffin down on him forever – something Mary knew *she* could never do if she were in the same position. At length Hilda appeared at the top of the last flight of stairs, some distance behind the coffin, accompanied by her brother, Tom. She was dressed completely in black – she had insisted on complete mourning – and the contrast with the extreme pallor of her face was startling. But her eyes were as hard and bright and searching as ever and her bearing calmly assured. She missed nothing as she descended the stairs, her eyes swiftly traversing the hall, the back hall, the sea of faces below her – Mary knew she could name all of them afterwards if asked – taking all in with that characteristic penetrating gaze. And then she was in the thronged hallway, nodding her head here and there, accepting the condolences of people with a cold formality, shaking hands, arranging about cars and who was to travel with whom, telling one of the maids not to forget about the fires while she was away, whispering to Mary to hurry and get her coat and sit with her in the car immediately behind the hearse. A marvel, thought Mary again, she was really a marvel, so coldly efficient when the mortal remains of her husband were disappearing into the maw of the hearse. And, for the third or fourth time since the death, Mary experienced a strange feeling of revulsion, a shrinking of her heart away, from this cold practicality in the presence of death. But the feeling vanished in a renewed surge of admiration for Hilda's iron bearing.

The cortège wound slowly down the road, the mourners on foot strung out immediately behind the hearse, a long line of cars crawling in their wake. Mary and Hilda sat stiffly upright on the back seat of the first car which was being driven by their brother, Tom, a taciturn middle-aged doctor who practised in the south of Ireland. When they started off, Mary, in an instinctive gesture of sympathy, put out her hand and caught Hilda's hand, and held it, pressing it gently now and then in silent commiseration. The church bell grew louder as they descended into the valley.

They were approaching the outskirts of the town: a huddle of small cottages, ugly detached villas, the bleak unlandscaped severity of a corporation housing-scheme. In many of the windows blinds were drawn; children peeped round the edges of half-open doors; a woman wiped her hands in her tattered apron, crossed herself, pushed four squealing boys in front of her into the house. Men paused on the pavement, raised their hats as the hearse passed, and vehicles halted. Dark withered leaves drifted slowly down on them like a macabre confetti of death and the bell rang still louder in their ears. The sun was lost behind a pall of smoke and the light turned lurid and faintly sinister as the funeral procession wound into the centre of the town.

Hilda still remained silent; Mary continued to hold her hand. Sometimes she could feel the nails of her sister's hand pressing into the flesh of her palm but Hilda's face was composed and her eyes, staring straight ahead, hard in the grey October light. She thought of Hilda as a child; of how she'd always seemed so clever and superior and masterful almost – she was 11 years older – of how she'd looked up to her always, as everyone seemed to do, deferred to her wisdom and understanding in everything; of how she'd wept with joy on learning of her engagement, poured out her heart to her in pages of rapturous congratulation; of how she'd saved for months, yes months, to buy her an expensive wedding present she couldn't really afford. People had talked that time but people would always talk. No matter what you did. William John had been older than her of course. A lot older. And people had said nasty things about her. Jealousy of course. Pure jealousy. And look how wrong they had been. Wrong. It had been a wonderful marriage. A happy marriage. Never had she heard Hilda complain. Never.

Then a shadow darkened her heart as she thought of how Hilda always seemed to take her loyalty for granted, accepting it so casually, with a sort of superior aloofness. She thought of the day she'd told Hilda of her own impending marriage; of how her sister had gradually brought the conversation round to money and position – then asked her point-blank how much Michael earned, what was his age and background; and of how she couldn't tell her what he earned because she didn't know or care; of how hurt she was and how she flushed and got embarrassed and suddenly hated her. Yes. Hated her sister. And then she thought of her mother who'd always called Hilda *The Deep One*. Yes. *The Deep One*. She tried to put these dark thoughts out of her mind, horrified at her disloyalty and impiety on an occasion like this, but she could not stop praying that Hilda would give some sign of sorrow, a gesture, a word, a tear, some sign from the heart. And then she thought of a poem she'd learned at school, and of a line in it about thoughts that lie too deep for tears, and this consoled her a little. Perhaps Hilda's grief was too deep for tears. But all the time she could hear her mother's gentle insistent voice. *The Deep One. The Deep One. The Deep One*.

They were passing through the centre of the town. Oncoming cars and lorries were halting, pedestrians stood bare-headed in respect, curious faces peeped round the edges of drawn shop-window blinds. A guard on point-duty stood to attention and saluted and an old shawled woman knelt on the pavement, her beads in her hands, her lips moving. At length they turned in through the entrance gates, crunching up the avenue over the loose sea-gravel to the wide-open church doors. The great throng of men – mostly workers from the factory – who had been following the remains on foot now gathered around the hearse as it drew to a halt.

A young curate, attended by an altar boy with a holy water stoup and a sprinkler, stood waiting in the church for the coffin. Tom got out and opened the door of the car for Hilda and Mary. Four selected young men from the factory had come forward to lift the coffin from the hearse and bear it up the aisle on their shoulders to its place in front of the main altar. Hilda and Mary followed the four bearers up the aisle, the priest's voice droning quietly in Latin, and the empty church began to fill up behind them. The four coffin-bearers, with the assistance of others, were now lowering the coffin into position on the catafalque outside the altar rails. Mary and Hilda and all the other chief mourners filed into the two front pews and when the priest's voice had droned to a halt and he had retreated into the sacristy to vest himself for Mass they knelt and waited. One of the undertaker's men came up and arranged mass-cards and wreaths on the lid of the coffin.

Mary looked at the massive coffin resting on the catafalque between four flickering candles. The coffin had made the bearers sweat and grunt with its weight, but she knew that the frail wasted corpse inside was as light as a bird. She thought of the dead man in his prime – if that was the word: he was old in her eyes from the first day she saw him – and realised with a shock that even then he was small and thin and frail, but the force of his personality, his extraordinary charm and youthful ways, his ruthless energy in business and pleasure, had contrived to create the image of a younger and bigger man. He had done all in his power to make Hilda happy and even if she had never quite reconciled herself to his frequent and sometimes mysterious business trips abroad, she could never chide him with neglect: no matter where he was, London, Paris, New York, he telephoned her every day. Only once had she heard of any unpleasantness between them: something about a letter written on scented paper that she received from him when he was abroad.

Mary recalled the last time she'd seen him alive, a few weeks ago, of how grieved she'd been to see that frail wasted body, hardly visible in outline under the bedclothes, the white shrunken face, the hoarse cracked whisper of a voice. His voice: that had been the most appalling thing of all. A voice that had been so resonantly authoritative, arrogant almost, to everyone – even to Hilda at times – in every corner of the house and factory. An old man, she'd thought, dying, dying, as she looked at the emaciated body beneath the bedclothes.

A cold shiver of revulsion ran through her and she prayed that Hilda would weep – there was nothing like tears in a situation like this – that death would soften her heart so that she could take her in her arms and comfort her. She kept on imploring God for some sign from Hilda: something to hold back the bitter tide that was rising in her heart: a tenderness of movement, an inflection of the voice, a tear. But Hilda continued to sit stiffly upright, unbending, staring straight ahead, her eyes hard and bright and unyielding.

The young priest, vested in black, strode out from the sacristy followed by two altar boys in faded white surplices and black soutanes. He was handsome and fresh-faced, Mary noticed for the first time, and vigorous in his movements. There was a great clatter as the Mass began and the congregation knelt to pray. But Mary noticed that Hilda had not even opened her missal and her rosary hung motionlessly from her hands.

Dear God, Mary prayed, watching the engrossed priest at the altar, help me to comfort Hilda in her great affliction. I *know* Hilda is good, kind, charitable, I know this. I know she had a happy married life, even if her wish to have children was never granted. She's my sister. My only sister. I *know* her. I know she is all these things. But, please God, let her give me some sign that her heart is touched, that she mourns for this man who, after all, was her husband for 25 years and indulged her every whim. *Please*, God. Mary tried to pray like this but the words seemed to get clogged up in her mind, jumbled together, and every time the priest intoned the sonorous Latin phrases aloud he seemed to be repeating: "The Deep One! The Deep One!" It was terrible. Terrible.

The Mass was over and, with an outburst of coughing, the kneeling congregation rose noisily and sat, waiting for the panegyric which the young priest had now come forward to the altar rails to deliver. The priest clasped his hands across his stomach, cleared his throat, waiting for the last coughs and shuffles to subside and then, glancing in Hilda's direction for a moment, he began to speak. Somewhere at the back of the church a prayer-book or a handbag clattered to the floor and he frowned.

He spoke with assurance but without variety of tone in a flat cold voice that at times reminded Mary of a child reading from a story-book. Sometimes, for a moment, he joined the tips of his extended fingers across his breast in an inverted V, but he always returned his hands to their clasped position across his stomach. It was a conventional eulogy: an outstanding man and an outstanding Catholic, a man whose word was his bond and whose life was pervaded by a deep and generous charity; a man who headed every public and private subscription list and who was a model employer; a man whose deep faith was as strong as his devotion to family life; a man of integrity and principle whose death would leave a great void in the community; their hearts would go out to his widow in her great loss.

The priest finished speaking and strode back into the sacristy. A sudden expectant hush fell on the congregation; this was the moment for which they had all been waiting: would the clergy attempt to collect offerings over the remains of William John in spite of his known wishes? Even Mary, who as a Dubliner of long standing – where the custom did not exist – felt little sense of involvement in the delicate issues at stake, was conscious of a feeling of tension in herself: she was aware of how much the Canon was opposed to the creation of a precedent. The church was enveloped in an intense watchful silence; minutes ticked by; a car back-fired outside and the noise was like a peal of thunder; boards creaked as people shifted the weight of their bodies; the sound of loud voices and doors banging from the direction of the sacristy seemed an almost profane intrusion. Mary felt that a thousand eyes were boring into her back. She could see a film of sweat on Hilda's upper lip, the tense rigidity of her body.

A great audible gasp rose from the congregation as two altar boys emerged from the sacristy carrying the small wooden table used in the collection of offerings. They placed it at the altar rails and returned to the sacristy. Another great gasp rose as the Canon walked out into the sanctuary. A rustle of movement, a whisper of excited voices, swept the crowded pews and then there was uniform silence. The Canon stood some way back from the wooden table and faced the congregation. He was an old man, tall and lean, but he held himself erect with an almost military air: he had been an army chaplain in his early years. His pale thin face wore a look of stern composure but the nervous strain he was undergoing revealed itself in two tiny spots of red on his normally colourless cheeks. He made no attempt to speak.

Suddenly one of William John's brothers, who was sitting further along the seat from Hilda, moved over to her and began to whisper. In the intense silence Mary could hear every word.

"We're not having offerings, isn't that right, Hilda? *He* said that and we stick to it, what?"

Hilda nodded her assent with quick movements of her head.

"Well, then we'll sit it out for a while", he went on grimly, "because no one will pay till we pay first. And we won't pay." He went back to his place.

Another spasm of unrest convulsed the congregation and then plunged it into the same vigilant silence. The Canon, who had been watching the exchange of words between Hilda and William John's brother, now realised that the chief mourners were not going to give way and anger took hold of him: the flush on his cheeks deepened and expanded and his lips were drawn into a thin tight line. He glanced furiously in the direction of Hilda and the other principal mourners for a moment, then turned and walked into the sacristy. The two altar boys carried the wooden table after him. Another wave of movement and voices swept through the church. Mary could see a faint smile of triumph on the lips of William John's two brothers, but Hilda's face was still white and tense. Mary's heart went out to her.

In a few moments the Canon re-appeared on the altar followed by two altar boys, one of whom bore a thurible, the other a holy-water stoup and a sprinkler. The flush had gone from the Canon's face but his lips were still drawn in a firm thin line. He came through the altar gates to the coffin, followed by the two altar boys, and immediately began reading in Latin in a quick low voice. Three times he sprinkled holy water on the coffin and three times he incensed it with the thurible. Then the congregation rose to its feet, the undertaker's assistant swiftly collected the mass-cards and wreaths, and the coffin was hoisted up on the shoulders of the four bearers – William John's two brothers and two men from the factory – and, led by the Canon, still intoning in Latin, borne down the aisle to the door. At that point the Canon and altar boys went back to the sacristy. Mary grasped Hilda's right arm as they followed the remains.

The graveyard was in the church grounds, a hummocky wilderness of long grass and untended graves through which the coffin-bearers had to pick their steps with care. One of them stumbled on a large loose stone hidden in the grass and Mary could see the sweat running down his forehead, the knotted veins standing out on his temples, as some men rushed forward to help him. They were approaching the site of the grave, around which four grave-diggers were standing ready, and the wet slabs of newly-turned earth gleamed in the thin autumn sunshine. Below them, in the distance, the sea was a metallic grey, cold, desolate, and behind them a stunted huddle of exposed trees, stripped of all leaves, crouched away from the ocean and the prevailing wind. It was cold and bare in the graveyard and there was no heat in the sun.

Mary began to feel the cold creeping into her limbs as she helped Hilda over the rough uneven ground towards the edge of the grave. The four coffin-bearers were gently lowering the coffin across two ropes stretched out beside the grave. Hilda's lips, Mary noticed, were faintly tinged with purple and her face was ashen. The cold was affecting her as well. Both of them now stood at the edge of the grave, eyes downcast, gloved hands folded together. Slowly, silently, people began to gather about the open grave, jostling one another gently, taking up vantage points on hummocks of earth and on other graves, watching the principal mourners, the coffin, the gaping pit. Sometimes a person detached himself from the crowd, went over to another grave, knelt and prayed.

There was a movement at the edge of the crowd, people drew aside, and the Canon came into view followed by an altar boy with a holy-water stoup and a sprinkler. He walked to the edge of the grave, opposite Mary and Hilda, opened a book and commenced to read in Latin. His voice was lost in the open spaces of the graveyard and Mary could barely hear him; she closed her eyes and tried to pray. A sound made her open them again. The grave-diggers were lowering the coffin into the grave by means of the two lengths of rope. The coffin swayed a little on its descent, the men paying out the rope very slowly; it struck the sides of the grave with a hollow thud, dislodging clay and stones that trickled and fell to the bottom with a sound that resembled the scurrying of rats. When the coffin came to rest on the bottom the grave-diggers pulled up their ropes.

A thin cold wind had now crept up from the sea. The wind ruffled the sparse white hairs of the Canon, riffled the pages of his book, carried his words a little louder across the open grave and the coffin to Hilda and Mary: "It was from dust that thou wert made and into dust thou shalt return." He spoke in English for the first time and the words froze Mary's heart. Now he was scattering stones and clay into the grave with a shovel one of the grave-diggers had handed him and sprinkling holy water. Some of the stones struck the coffin with a hollow rattle and a few lumps of clay broke and scattered over the lid. The sound of the stones striking the coffin and the thin fouling of clay on the lid sent a cold shiver of mingled fear and pity through Mary's body. This was the most dreadful moment of all. Then she became conscious of a new movement in Hilda's body and a low barely-perceptible sound: almost a moan. She looked at her sister. Hilda was weeping: tears were streaming down her cold white cheeks towards her thin purple-tinged lips, and she was rooting in her handbag for a handkerchief.

Dear God, wept Mary to herself, at long last it has happened: a sign! How she had prayed for this moment! How she wished she could take her sister in her arms and comfort her at this terrible moment of desolation. Poor dear Hilda!

The four grave-diggers, coatless, their shirt sleeves rolled up, now began to fill in the grave, working swiftly under the critical gaze of the onlookers. Again there was the hollow sound of stones striking the coffin and the clatter of damp earth, but soon the coffin disappeared from sight and there was only the sound of the shovels striking against stones and grating into gravelly earth and the low sound of Hilda's sobs. The Canon waited, and the grave-diggers, the grave now filled in and levelled off, were laying down their shovels. Their armpits were dark with sweat and sweat too lay damply on their brows and they were breathing heavily.

The Canon knelt and the people began to kneel also. He asked them to pray for the eternal repose of the soul of William John Lynam. Mary helped Hilda to find a flat stone on which to kneel. She found another stone for herself and she noticed that her legs were so numb that she could not feel the cold of the stone. They all prayed with the priest and their voices rose thinly into the cold air of the graveyard. Then the Canon rose and left. The people, too, rose stiffly to their feet, men put on their hats and caps, little groups began to gossip for a moment or two, broke up, and then they drifted slowly towards the gate. A line of people waited to sympathise with Hilda who was weeping quietly into her handkerchief. And then Mary touched her sister gently on the arm, grasped it firmly, and led her slowly towards the gate.

When they reached Tom's car he wasn't there – Mary saw him talking to someone in the distance – but the car was unlocked. She opened one of the back doors for Hilda and then got in beside her.

"Oh Hilda!" Mary cried out, unable to suppress her emotion any longer, "poor dear Hilda!" She threw her arms around her sister, who was also weeping, and drew her towards her. "You poor poor thing you! I know how you feel and how much you'll miss him, he was so good and straight and true! I know, dear Hilda, how hard it is! I can just picture myself in your position and know exactly how you feel! Pray for him", wept Mary, "pray for him, Hilda!"

Slowly Hilda disentangled herself from Mary's embrace. She was still sobbing but her eyes were dry. Mary continued to hold one of her hands even though Hilda had drawn away from her.

"I'm not crying for him", said Hilda, her sobs subsiding, her eyes cold and hard as the tombstones stretching away in front of them, "not for him."

Mary recoiled from her, relinquishing her hand, wide-eyed, shocked. Hilda dabbed at her tearless eyes with her handkerchief.

"Not for him, Hilda?" asked Mary weakly after a long silence.

"No", replied Hilda, rummaging in her handbag for her compact, then suddenly looking up from the bag straight into Mary's eyes. "After all, I was only *one* of the women in his life." She paused but continued to stare at Mary. "You never knew that, did you?"

Mary shook her head. Suddenly she found herself floundering in very deep water and she struggled to keep her head above the currents now swirling all around her. The elderly maids, those mysterious trips abroad, these things at once took on a new significance. She felt ashamed of her blindness and naivety and tried to put her chaotic thoughts in order.

"But surely", she said, "after all these years you must have cared a *little* for him?" She thought of her own happy marriage: she wanted Hilda to say that *some* of her tears had been shed for him.

"To care and to love are two different things", said Hilda: there was no comfort for her there.

"Then it was true what people said at the time?" she asked.

"That I was marrying him for his money?"

Mary nodded.

"Of course it was true", said Hilda, inspecting her face in the mirror of her compact.

It had begun to rain: heavy sporadic drops splattered themselves in strawberry patterns against the windscreen, drummed on the roof of the car.

Mary stared at her sister as if she had never seen her before. As if they were meeting for the first time. All those years she had shut her ears against the gossip about Hilda's marriage, even reprimanded her mother, and now it was true. *The Deep One*. Yes. Her mother had been right. What a terrible fool she had been: she could see that *now*.

"You've always been so innocent, haven't you, Mary?" Hilda stopped powdering her nose, looked at her sister.

"Maybe . . . maybe I have . . ." Mary didn't know what to say but she thought of that time once before when she had hated her sister. And suddenly she hated her now again. Hated her for what she'd done and because she seemed somehow to be calling Michael's love for her into question, to be calling all love into question. Now every time Michael went off on a business trip for a few days she'd be suspicious. She could see herself inspecting his underwear closely, smelling his shirts, on his return. She thought of the hollow sound the stones made rattling on the coffin: the world was full of hollow people. Even her own sister. And then she remembered how in the end Hilda had wept and suddenly all hatred drained from her and her heart reached out to her sister again. After all, apart from Michael and the children, Hilda was all she had in the world.

"But Hilda", she blurted out, "you were crying . . . crying . . ."

"I was crying for myself", said Hilda, putting away her compact, snapping her handbag shut, "for all those wasted loveless years."

The sisters stared at each other and suddenly Mary began to weep, tears began to stream down her cheeks, her body shook with deep convulsive sobs, she couldn't restrain herself, she wept with the abandon of a child. Hilda caught one of her hands, pressed it, put an arm round her shoulder and drew her sister to her and now she was weeping on Hilda's breast. Uncontrollably. Hilda, her face impassive, her eyes still tearless, continued to hold her sister in her arms until Tom came and drove them away through torrents of slanting rain.

The above story was written was in the 1960s and is published here for the first time. Along with eight other published or broadcast stories, it is included in Francis Harvey's unpublished manuscript, The Way Things Were Then. *(Editor's Note: publishers, take cognizance!)*

Francis Harvey, a poet and fiction-writer, was born in Enniskillen in 1925. He is the author of five collections of poetry, most recently The Boa Island Janus *(1996),* Making Space *(2000) and* Collected Poems *(2006), all from The Dedalus Press. He lives in Donegal Town, Co Donegal.*

TWO POEMS

Gerard Smyth

ONE EVENING AFTER SONGS OF PRAISE

It was our first home, built on ground
that belonged to ghosts,
on a height that in January caught the first snows,
that in June came alive when it became
a place for outings on golden evenings,
for *hide-and-seek* and *finders keepers*.

The house settled, absorbed new sounds:
a stereo playing *New Kid in Town*,
the easeful kettle coming to the boil,
banging doors, the rattle of cups,
our firstborn speaking first words in his high chair.

One evening after *Songs of Praise*
I stepped out into the cul-de-sac, lifted my gaze
and saw the lights come on in upper windows,
the glow of televisions.
Out of the dusk-fragrance, the eerie calm,
a voice called the names of children lingering
in one last game of *catch-me-if-you-can*.

BLACK FLAGS

The names of internees appeared on walls.
Instant memorials, sprayed on mysteriously.
The Lagan and the Liffey, those rivers
were moving faster like rivers with a purpose.
From northern windows black flags fluttered.
First there were prayers of intercession,
then prayers of requiem for old young men.
They were marionettes pale from not seeing the sun,
weak from carrying the darkness that covered them.
And after summer lost its strength
the black flags hung in abandonment, dissipating
until they became ghosts of themselves
in country lanes, over farms and meadows.
Or fallen like the battle-corpses in Whitman's epic.

Gerard Smyth works as a journalist with The Irish Times. *He is the author of six collections of poems, most recently* The Mirror Tent *(Dedalus Press, 2007). He lives in Dublin.*

SECRETARY OF THE TIMES

David Edgar

Superglued to the zeitgeist.

When I was three and three-quarters, my parents first took me to the theatre. The play was *Beauty and the Beast* by Nicholas Stuart Grey, and at the first entrance of the masked and fearsome creature, I screamed the place down. Eventually, my behaviour became so disruptive that I had to be removed from the auditorium, and as, conveniently, my aunt was administrator of the theatre, I was escorted backstage to meet the now maskless beast in his dressing room, to shake his hand, to watch him put his mask on again, to shake his hand a second time, and to be taken back into the auditorium. Thus reassured, on his next entrance, I screamed the place down.

I have had good experiences in the theatre since, but none quite like that. A year later I went to the same playhouse to see the same author's *Tinder Box* – a play full of sinister witches and huge dogs. But this time I was wise. I'd realised it was illusion. And I'd realised also that there was nothing in the world I wanted to do more than helping to make those illusions. From the day the magic died – or more accurately, the day I realised that it was magic – I wanted to be up there with the magicians.

Between the ages of 13 and 19, however, I found my ambitions somewhat narrowed. Following a disastrous school performance as Miss Prism in *The Importance of Being Earnest* – personally I blame the shoes – my mother concluded "well, it's not going to be acting, is it, dear". In subsequent years I realised – or was informed – that it was unlikely to be designing, directing nor stage management either. I came to writing, therefore, by process of elimination, it being – among other advantages, like being indoor work with no heavy lifting – the only theatrical craft which didn't involve daily interaction with other people.

There is a third defining date in my history. I was 20, and thus in my second year at university, in 1968, a dawn in which it was bliss to be alive, but to be young and in full-time higher education was very heaven. My experience of the worldwide student revolt of the late 1960s gave me a mission for my work as a playwright which has continued, through various processes of revision, up to the present day. When I left university, even more when I left a short career in journalism three years later, I knew that I wanted to be a playwright of a particular kind. I wanted to be part of a tradition of politically engaged playwriting that ran back to Bernard Shaw and was dominated by the legacy of Bertolt Brecht, but which was also central to the project of the British theatre which began on 8 May 1956, with the opening of John Osborne's groundbreaking play *Look Back in Anger* at the Royal Court theatre.

There are two more important dates. If you reverse the last two digits of my birth year – as Orwell did to find his most famous title – you get 1984, the year of the last great miners' strike whose defeat signalled, if any single event did, the death of the dream of a renewed revolutionary socialism that began in 1968. While if you upend '68, literally, turn the figures upside down, you get the date of the great counter-revolution of Eastern Europe during which millions of young people used political tools forged 21 years earlier to overthrow the regimes which claimed to be the torchbearers of the communist ideal.

I believe that these and other great events of the last 52 years – including events that occurred on this island – have been more consistently, rigorously and durably represented in theatre than anywhere else. Of course, there have been peaks and troughs, periods when television drama or the novel appeared to speak more prominently for the times. But taken as a whole, from kitchen sink drama to verbatim theatre, I think theatre in general, and new plays in particular, have been (in Balzac's phrase) the most effective secretary of the times.

To say that not everyone agrees with this is a triumph of understatement. A month or so ago critic Max Wolf wrote in *The Observer* that there were no new plays in the West End any more. Hardly a surprise: you can hardly open the arts pages of the papers without reading articles about the death of text-based theatre. The Arts Council of England has dropped new writing as a priority for funded companies in its theatre policy, emphasising circus and street arts in its stead. And if this provokes a sense of *déjà vu*, it should: as, God knows, we have been here before.

I started in the theatre in the very late sixties, a period in which, after perhaps the most dazzling period of British new writing of the twentieth century, new work seemed in the doldrums. Then as now, the obituaries for new writing were written. Then as now, pundits held up performance work as the wave of the future. In fact, of course, what was happening was not a terminal decline in new writing but a dip, as one wave of new playwrights paused for breath and another was preparing to launch itself on the scene.

It seems clear to me that the Royal Court dramatists of the fifties and early sixties shared not only a theatre but also a subject: the plays of Osborne, Arnold Wesker, John Arden and the early Edward Bond all confront the continued resilience of the British class system. The generation that followed, my generation, was forged in the youth revolt of the late sixties and enabled by the abolition of theatre censorship in 1968 to expand both its content and its forms, out of traditional theatre buildings and into clubs, pubs, studio theatres and the streets. The spirit of that period was brought home to me most vividly by a particular event. I lived in the late sixties and early seventies in Bradford, which for reasons best known to itself had won the North of England franchise of the late sixties counterculture, and which played host to veritable gardens of exotic theatrical flowers during the two immensively successful Bradford Festivals of 1970 and 1971. (So successful were they, by the by, with so many people having such an obviously wonderful time, that the City authorities refused to finance a third, on the grounds that giving so many people so much unambiguous pleasure was clearly a gross abuse of public funds.) Here, you would find performance artists careering around the city on pink bicycles ridden in Red Arrow formation; there, my friend Howard Brenton's play *Scott of the Antarctic* was being performed in the ice rink, with myself essaying the small but nonetheless significant role of the Almighty; while, somewhere else, Portable Theatre was presenting an early play by David Hare or Snoo Wilson, as like as not involving loud bangs and dead dogs, the Welfare State troupe was enacting a pagan child's naming ceremony – with fire-eaters and real goats – in the Wool Exchange, and Albert Hunt's Art College Group was staging a full-scale mock-up of an American Presidential election, with live elephant, in the streets of the city. And, somewhere else again, in clubs and pubs, agitprop groups with names like Red Ladder were relating contemporary labour history, and joining, in their own way, the general and universal call for the overthrow of all fixed things.

Among them was my group, called after Rousseau The General Will, for whom I wrote five agitprop plays during the period of the 1970 to 1974 Conservative Government. As the seventies went on, however, I grew increasingly disillusioned with this sort of play. In the early seventies, international politics was dominated by the certainties of the Vietnam War and domestic policy by what seemed an equally life-and-death struggle between a Conservative government and a newly militant industrial working class – and that's not to mention what was happening here. After the miners brought down the government in 1974, however, it became ever clearer that the revolutionary potential of the situation had been overestimated, and as workers' militancy faded, other issues began to appear. The problem is that, while you can deal with wars and strikes through agitprop, the issues raised by feminism and anti-racism involve the interface between the objective and the subjective, the political and the personal. So you need to show recognisable people behaving in a recognisable way, rather than cartoon characters. I wasn't alone in this feeling. True, there remained agitprop companies committed to seeking a working-class audience outside theatre buildings, but others sought to make a career in the mainstream theatre, moving away from the streets and on to the stages of the great institutional theatres in London: the Royal Court, the Royal Shakespeare Company and the National Theatre.

The political plays of the seventies – written by such as David Hare, Trevor Griffiths, Howard Brenton, Barry Keeffe, Howard Barker and me – became known as "state of England plays" because they shared a model of what had made England what it was.

In essence, Hare's *Plenty*, about the diplomatic service, Brenton's *The Churchill Play*, commenting on the increasing authoritarianism of the British state during the Heath Government, and my *Destiny* about the rise of the NF in seventies England pursued elements of a single grand narrative which very roughly went like this: the UK had been on the right side in the war against Hitler, but had squandered its moral capital afterwards. There'd been a chance after the war to create a genuine egalitarian, emancipatory socialism, but it was implemented too half-heartedly by the 1945-51 Labour government and the opportunity was lost. The country then held a kind of party in the fifties and sixties, squandering its post-imperial riches, and in the seventies had gone into freefall decline, at the end of which, it was assumed, final collapse would occur and "true socialism" would emerge phoenix-like from the ashes.

And of course, something new did indeed emerge at the end of the seventies, but it sure as hell wasn't true socialism. But as the iron certainties of class politics frayed and withered, a new generation of playwrights appeared, addressing the issues of identity and difference. In the seventies, it seemed compulsory for political playwrights to answer to names like Howard, David or John. In the eighties, they were just as likely to be called things like Charlotte, Sharman, Bryony and Clare. In 1979, there were two currently-writing, nationally-known women writers in Britain (Pam Gems and Caryl Churchill). A decade later there were two dozen.

Although by definition very different to the two previous waves, the new women writers too addressed one of the dominant questions of contemporary life, in conversation with an audience whose lives were being changed by it. There was also, though to a lesser extent, an upsurge of new writing – again, including many women writers – expressing other ethnic, regional and national identities. As with the previous waves, the peak of the early to mid-eighties was followed by a predictable dip, when the seemingly exponential growth of new women's writing came to a temporary halt. But in this case the dip was combined with a decline of new play production (down from around 15% of the 1970-85 repertoire to around 7%), cutbacks in subsidy to small-scale theatre and the reps, and a dramatic narrowing of the mainstream theatre repertoire, increasingly confined to adaptations, twentieth-century warhorses, not always unjustly neglected classics (performed on dangerously raked stages), interminable late Chekhov (*plus ça change*) and a shrinking circle of sure-fire Shakespearian pops.

Predictably, all of this led many to declare the theatre text dead. Then as now, critics mourned the decline in new writing, and prominent up-and-coming directors described living playwrights as, variously, exploitative, untrustworthy, inadequate, sectarian and sanctimonious (the last two being Stephen Daldry, but, then, he'd just been appointed artistic director of the Royal Court, so he had to be polite). By 1995, and despite mainstream theatre landmarks like David Hare's trilogy of plays about British institutions at the National, critics and directors were in agreement that the individually written new play was as redundant as the slide rule or the typewriter.

In fact, of course, this was rubbish. The explosion of new writing in the mid-nineties – the movement known, variously, as the Bratpack, in-yer-face theatre, smack and spunk theatre, the New Brutalism and, on the other side of the channel, new European drama – put theatre up there with pop, fashion, fine art and food as the fifth leg of the new Cool Britannia, and not for revivals of Lopa de Vega or deconstructions of *Measure for Measure*. Even more striking was the way Sarah Kane and Mark Ravenhill's work in particular spread like a flashfire across continental Europe. Like any regular theatre traveller, I now know the words for "Blasted", "Shopping", "Fucking" and "Psychosis" in all of the languages of the expanded EU.

As is well known, in-yer-face theatre was characterised by being largely about young people, possessed of a cool and sheeny style, and containing the representation of explicit sex, drug-use and violence. Many of these plays also shared a subject, which was, indeed, the dominant theatre subject of the time. It seems unanswerable that the plays of the mid-nineties address masculinity and its discontents as demonstrably as the plays of the early sixties addressed class and those of the seventies the failures of social democracy. Insofar as masculinity touches on economic, cultural and social issues – most particularly violence and militarism – it is a political subject. Certainly, Sarah Kane's *Blasted*, in which a coercive relationship between an older man and a younger woman is transformed – metaphorically and literally – into a Balkan warzone is one example of how in-yer-face drama recharts the relationship between the personal and the political. In-yer-face drama is political in another way. Because Mark Ravenhill writes about a generation which can't see beyond next Tuesday or back past last weekend, it doesn't mean he likes it. Among other things, *Shopping and Fucking* is an elegy for lost political certainties. In Ravenhill's underestimated *Some Explicit Polaroids*, an AIDS victim who is refusing to take the medication which will save his life, admits: "I want Communism and apartheid. I want the finger on the nuclear trigger. I want the gay plague. I want to know where I am". Similarly, Gregory Burke's *Gagarin Way*, is about a group of articulate but incompetent anti-globalisation protesters whose ham-fisted and finally disastrous capture of a company boss is consciously evocative of the bold political activism of an earlier era. Far from celebrating the death of radical politics, it seems to me that one of the great subjects of in-yer-face theatre is mourning its loss.

It would have been a surprise if, unlike the previous waves, a movement with its finger so obviously superglued to the zeitgeist would go on for ever. There is no doubt that, after Sarah Kane's suicide in February 1999, in-yer-face theatre suffered a decline. By the turn of the millennium, the increasing dominance of new plays about young people shooting up and sounding off in South London flats led to a justified suspicion that a theatre that sought to diagnose the crisis of masculinity was now merely a symptom of it; that a drama which sought to mourn the end of politics has biodegraded into a drama which demonstrates it. And, predictably, the buzzards started gathering. In May 2001, the Arts Council produced a policy document (*The Next Stage*) backed up by an unusually authoritative report by a consultancy (Peter Boyden Associates) into the roles and functions of English Regional Producing Theatres. There were highly welcome elements in the Boyden report, in that it confirmed once and for all that the 30% drop in regional theatre attendance in the nineties had had something to do with a 50% rise in seat prices, a superficially self-evident proposition which many theatre managers found it hard to grasp, but which the National Theatre's ten-pound Olivier season has triumphantly proved.

But, in addition, Boyden had views on the repertoire. For him, English theatre remained dangerously wedded to a postwar age and a core canon which the public no longer knows, citing an inexorably widening "spectacle gap between subsidised theatre and sophisticated mixed-media, event-based culture". By contrast "text-based drama is in relative decline".

The recommendations arising out of this analysis were given an exaggerated spin when leaked to *The Daily Telegraph*: there was talk of theatres being told to mount laser, video and acrobatic spectacles as a condition of public grants. Strenuously denied, there is nonetheless a thrust both in the report and even more in the Arts Council's response *The Next Stage* against straight plays and in favour of a theatre that accepts "a multi-cultural, digital and regional Britain", acknowledging that this means embracing "a wider range of forms and traditions". Behind both reports is an assumption that text-based work is nostalgic and dusty, while non-text based work is up-to-the-minute, trendy and popular. Although never stated, it's pretty clear that what the report's authors meant by non-text-based work was not rock concerts and gymnastic displays but work by those site-specific, devising, visually-based performance companies whose work is promoted so vigorously by some critics, and most of the drama departments of British universities. There's a parlour game in which you imagine what the Olivier award shortlist would look like if it was drawn up by the people who run the Turner Prize – if left up to the British Theatre Academy, top place in the annual theatre awards would be a tussle between Desperate Optimists and Forced Entertainment.

While now, seven years on from *The Next Stage*, the new Arts Council of England theatre policy makes clear that, whatever they meant at the time, the funders now do want to encourage fire-eaters and clowns at the expense of text. The 2007-2011 theatre policy statement drops new writing from its production priorities in favour of giving "particular emphasis to experimental practice and interdisciplinary practice, circus and street arts".

Whereas I think that, once again, death of new theatre writing has been much exaggerated. It's too early to look back on the new writing of the noughts with the analytical confidence that we look back on the earlier waves of new writing, in the late fifties, the early seventies, the early eighties and the mid-nineties. But it's clear that 9/11 gave new writing a new subject. It's also clear that there is a particular form – fact-based theatre – that has emerged from the need to address the questions raised by the wars on terror and Iraq.

Several explanations have been put forward for this phenomenon. Two are almost tautological: the first is that theatre-as-journalism is literally that: in plays like – in particular – David Hare's play about railway privatisation, *The Permanent Way*, theatre is doing the kind of investigative, analytical job on the contemporary world that conventional journalism is failing to do, that, in particular, theatre is occupying space abandoned by traditional television documentary, trampled under the tank-tracks of reality TV. The second, connected argument is that despite notable exceptions like Antonia Bird's *The Hamburg Cell* (about the 9/11 bombers) and Peter Kosminsky's *The Government Inspector* (about David Kelly), most television drama-documentary has become corrupted by the requirements of genre (too much drama) and a sloppy attitude to research (not enough doc). Over the last couple of years, indeed, the generic television dramadoc has biodegraded into a dubious retelling of titbit political and royal sex scandals (the disclaimer for a 2005 drama about Princess Margaret was "some of the following is based on fact – and some isn't").

The third explanation is that fact-based drama is merely the form of a current renewal of political theatre, that, in essence, we're back in the 1970s. One good way of mapping post-9/11 political drama is to place it on a spectrum, calibrated according to its strict fidelity to fact. On the one end, there is strict verbatim theatre, like the series of edited dramatizations of significant trials and tribunals at the Tricycle Theatre in North London, most recently of the Saville Inquiry into Bloody Sunday. Then there are factual plays like Victoria Brittain and Gillian Slovo's Tricycle play *Guantanamo: Honour Bound to Defend Freedom*, based on edited interviews with prisoners, their relatives and lawyers, and the public record of statements by politicians. Other interview-based plays include Robin Soans' *Arab-Israeli Cookbook*, presented at the Gate and the Tricycle, the same author's *Talking to Terrorists* (at the Royal Court and on tour), and indeed *The Permanent Way*. Further along the spectrum lies David Hare's *Stuff Happens*, which joined up the dots of the events from the 9/11 attacks through and beyond the Iraq invasion, in the manner of traditional television drama-documentary, while Peter Morgan's *Frost/Nixon* is more in the model of television documentary-drama (including his own), in which a strong, archetypal narrative is imposed on a historical event. Further out again are the satirical plays of Alistair Beaton, presenting loosely fictionalised versions of public figures in satirical treatments of subjects like spin-doctoring and royal marriages. While, on the far opposite end of the spectrum to verbatim theatre, writers have been creating plays in which the global and domestic issues raised by the war on terror and Iraq are confronted by representative but fictional characters, set against the background of real contemporary events. Such plays include Roy Williams' recent play for the RSC about British troops in Iraq, *Days of Significance*. Finally, there is the form I call faction, in which a number of phenomena are conflated and fictionalised in order to present a thesis about their underlying characteristics. This form has the longest pedigree: it includes Frank McGuinness' *Someone to Watch Over Me*, a factionalised version of the Beirut hostage story, David Hare's *An Absence of War*, about a generic Labour election failure, and my own *The Shape of the Table*, *The Prisoner's Dilemma* and *Playing with Fire*, which were factional abstractions of the East European anti-communist revolutions of 1989, the international peace processes of the mid-1990s, and the 2001 riots in Oldham, Burnley and Bradford.

So the Life of Mars reading of what's happening now is persuasive. But there's other ways of looking at it. One is historical. It's worth remembering, that, once again, we have been here before. In the fifties and early sixties, the international Theatre of Fact school built plays out of documents, particularly trial transcripts. However, the theory behind these works was very precisely *not* to explain the phenomena they described. The idea of using documents as opposed to dramatic invention was a kind of abdication: it was saying, after the enormities of Auschwitz and Hiroshima, the old concepts of cause and effect no longer apply. All the playwright can do is present the documents, naked and unadorned, and you can make what you will of them. In this sense, Theatre of Fact is the other side of the coin of fifties' and sixties' absurdism. Both of them sought to express a world they could no longer analyse.

Superficially, verbatim theatre doesn't appear a direct or even bastard descendant of Theatre of Fact in that sense. Of all people, David Hare has not abandoned his mission to explain. But I wonder if, in the deliberate anti-theatricality of the Tricycle tribunals, and the minimalism of Robin Soans' reportage, there isn't an element of, if not abdication, then a desire to present a rather wider configuration of dots for the audience to try and join up. The point about faction is that it's a way of presenting a thesis unencumbered by factual specifics. One advantage of verbatim theatre is that you present factual specifics unencumbered by a thesis. As so many of these plays have the conflict between the West and Islam at their core, maybe some of them are expressing the confusions and agonies that most progressive people feel as they face down the choice between neo-liberal adventurism and Islamic fundamentalism. Interestingly, increasingly, verbatim theatre is not just sourced from interviews but about interviews. Aleky Blythe's *Come Out Eli* – a play about an East London siege in which the actors literally have earpieces on which the original interviews are played during the performance – is as much about the process as the product (indeed, it's top-and-tailed by a reproduction of negotiations between Blythe and a key witness who's only prepared to give an interview in exchange for sex). Similarly, Robin Soans' *Talking to Terrorists* seemed more about the contrast between the domestic lives and personal mannerisms of its interviewees and the enormity of their subject matter than it was about terrorism (in that sense, it could have been *Talking to Environmentalists* or *Talking to Drug-Dealers).* Increasingly, the Tricycle tribunals have been as much about the contrast between the coolness of the inquisitive form and the heat of the events they seek to explicate as about reportage; the dramatisation of the MacPherson inquiry, *The Colour of Justice*, was all about the inadequacies of contesting narratives of the same event. While the latest Tricycle tribunal play – *Called to Account* – gave the usual editing treatment to a fake trial of Tony Blair for war crimes; and Dennis Kelly's *Taking Care of Baby*, co-produced by Birmingham and Hampstead earlier this year, is a stage version of television mockumentary, an entirely fictional work about a woman wrongly imprisoned for murdering her baby, which effectively fools the audience for at least half its length (and for some members of the audience I was part of, much longer than that) that it is a real verbatim drama based on interviews about a real case.

So, theatre is both addressing important contemporary content but doing so in a form which challenges the provenance and privilege of the narratives which shape our perceptions. As I say, I think it is doing so because the increasing formal confusion of television fact-based drama – and its all-too-frequent imprisonment within genre – prevents it from doing the same job. Once again, British theatre – and British new writing in particular – will survive a new wave of obituaries (whether penned by critics, practitioners or the Arts Council of England) by the simple expedient of finding something for it to do that no other storytelling medium cares to do or can do, and setting down to do it.

Finally, if I'm right, and British theatre has managed, over the years, to present a uniquely consistent and authoritative picture of contemporary public life, why is this so? The reasons include things I haven't mentioned: a pretty consistent tradition of what is uncomfortably called "applied theatre" – work in schools and prisons, work with communities. A week tomorrow I have a play, written for 120 local actors and involving upwards of 500 people in other roles – opening in Dorchester, which doesn't just promote community cohesion, but *is* community cohesion. Speaking here, it would be impolite not to celebrate the continued influence of great actors, directors but particularly writers from both parts of this island, from Brian Friel and Frank McGuinness via Anne Devlin, Christina Reid and Sebastian Barry to Conor McPherson and Enda Walsh. Most importantly, for all my criticisms, the Arts Council has enabled and sustained an institutional structure that presents the canon and new work, the excellent and the experimental (and much experimental excellence), the celebratory and the oppositional, is able to sustain careers over time and, frankly, keeps theatre-makers making theatre in this country, as opposed to making film and television here or abroad.

But finally, and specifically to theatre writing, I think it's because the waves of new writers – the angry young men of the fifties, the post-'68 revolutionaries of the seventies, the women playwrights of the eighties, the in-yer-face group in the nineties, the fact-based dramatists now – found themselves speaking to a new audience who were addressing issues – class mobility, left politics, gender, the crisis of masculinity, the challenge of terrorism – that were immediate and important to them, and which were best confronted in the shared, safe space of dramatic fiction. One recent example of that was the way in which young Asian women flocked in surprising numbers to the Birmingham Repertory Theatre studio – pre, post and during the amputated run of *Behzti* – to see plays which addressed their concerns about culture, sexuality, family and faith. But the most dramatic recent instance is Roy Williams' *Little Sweet Thing*, which, the night I saw it at the Birmingham Rep 900-seat main house, played to an audience which was three-quarters full and three-quarters black. Williams' story of a black ex-con who tries but fails to break free from a criminal sub-culture contained two white characters, both of which are threatened and bullied by black characters, whom they seek first to emulate and then to out-do. The idea that emulating black urban culture can turn weak nice people into strong nasty ones is a pretty brave notion for a black writer to express. I think if it had been expressed in an interview or an article it would have been rejected angrily. In the theatre, I heard the unmistakable hum of recognition all around me. Because its audiences understood the most basic thing about theatre, that it provides a site in which you can say things that are riskier and more extreme than the things you can say elsewhere, because what you say is not real but pretend.

So for all the arguments for the arts as part of the tourism industry (vital), as a tool of civic regeneration (essential), as an employment escalator (indisputable), and as a means of community cohesion (indispensable), the best argument for the arts is for what only the arts can do, which is to create an imaginary world in which we can learn things about being human you can't learn anywhere else. Six-year-old Lucy, goes the story, is in the infants' painting class, and the teacher asks her what she's going to paint today. "I'm going to paint God", announces Lucy. "But Lucy," says the teacher, "no one knows what God looks like." "They will," says Lucy, "just as soon as I've finished my picture."

This address was delivered on 8 November, 2007, in the Grand Opera House, Belfast, as part of "Art at the Heart", a conference organized by the Arts Council of Northern Ireland.

One of the leading figures in British theatre, David Edgar was born in Birmingham in 1948. He is the author of numerous plays, television adaptations, radio plays and screenplays, as well as literary journalism. His most recent plays are The Prisoner's Dilemma *(2001),* Playing with Fire *(2005) and* Testing the Echo *(2008). He is Professor of Playwrighting Studies at the University of Birmingham.*

IN A GRAVE TIME

Cathal Ó Searcaigh

SIÚL SLÉIBHE

Ceobháisteach;
 boladh cumhra
 ón aiteannach.

Sos sa chomhrá;
 fosclaíonn bachlóg
 ar an dreasóg

Mám lom romham;
 fuiseog glébhinn
 os mo chionn.

Níl ann anois
 ach a bheith beo;
 amach anseo

Aimscoidh mé
 cuspóir eile, treo
 éigin as an cheo . . .

Téim in aghaidh
 na síne, go díreach
 le bheith fliuch

MOUNTAIN TREK

Drizzles drench the skin
  furze exudes
  a fragrance

A lull in the conversation
  a bramble
  breaking into flower

A bare mountain pass looms ahead
  a lark above me sweet
  translucent

Living is all there is
  to do now.
  Later

We can find purpose
  pathways
  out of maze and mist

Entering the eye of the storm
  drenching yourself
  in it

AMHRÁN NA MAIDINE

Iarraim ar an mhaidin gealadh ar a bhfuil ag fás
ar a bhfuil ag feo, ar an tseilide a d'éalaigh lena bheo
ón nimh i measc na mbláth, ar an tseangán lena lód trom
ag tógáil an chnoic thar chlocha an chosáin, ar an chrann
ard duilliúrach ar shuíomh na bildeála atá ag sú isteach
an salú toite ón inneall tochailte is á chur amach úrghlan
in anáil ghlas a dhúthrachta, ar an éan a fhíonn snáithe óir
a chuid ceoil ó thor go tor, ar na rósanna, na girseachaí croíúla
ina gcuid sciortaí dearga á gcumhrú féin ag tóin an tí,
ar nóinín an tsúil órbhuí a tchí an chos a dhéanfas é a chloí.

Iarraim ar an tsolas tuirlingt ar a bhfuil geal,
ar a bhfuil gruama, ar shnas buí bróige, ar bhealadh
gruaige, ar bholadh bréan na sráide, ar thorthaí ag dul i mboige,
ar aghaidh bhán ar chúl fuinneoige, ar lucht bruíne na cearnóige,
ar bhainne cíche na mná atá ag cothú linbh ar an fhaiche, ar chailíní
oifige,
ar an ógfhear sa tsólann a d'inis domh gur mó de mhí na méala
ná de mhí na meala a bhí faighte aige ar leabaidh a phósta,
ar na turasóirí drochdhaiteacha i gclós thí an ósta, ar na páistí ocracha
lena gcuid málaí gliú ag stad na traenach, ar an bhia
atá á scaipeadh agam ar linn na lachan, ar ár n-arán laethúil, ar Dhia.

Iarraim ar an ghrian triall ar mhian mo chroí,
iarraim uirthi luí ar a leabaidh, é a mhuirniú ina géaga solais,
a bhéal a phógadh lena beola samhraidh, inse dó i dteas an cheana
gur é mo leas agus cé gur cuireadh de mo dhóchas mé
go gcreidim ina ghrá, ina mhéin shéimh shuailceach, ina leabaidh séin
agus dá bhrí sin go dtig liom, d'ainneoin na n-ainneoin, éirí as an
duibheagán,
as ifreann mo léin is an mhaidin seo a bheannú le dán . . .

MORNING SONG

I ask the morning to brighten all that grows
and withers; the snail that pulled through somehow,
The flowers all poisoned. Brighten the ant with its heavy load
Mountaineering among pavement pebbles. Brighten the tree's
Leafy erectness on the building site as it sucks in gunge
From the digger and breathes it out again fresh and clean
In green enthusiasm; brighten the bird that stretches its golden chord
From one tuneful bush to another, the roses, the cheerful girls
In their red skirts perfuming themselves at the lower end of the house;
The golden-eyed daisy that perceives the foot that's going to trample it.

I ask the light to descend on bright things
Struck gloomy, yellow shoe polish, the scent
Of hair, stink of streets, fruits that have grown limp,
The pallid face behind a window, yobbos fighting in the town square,
Milk flowing from the wet-nurse siting on the lawn, office girls,
The young man in the lounge who described his honeymoon
As honeydoom, no, it wasn't a bed of roses,
Tourists of uncertain hue in the hotel yard, waifs
With bags of glue at the train stop, our daily bread
That I scatter among ducks and deities.

I ask the sun to journey to my heart's desire,
Lie down with him, fondle his core with gold-lacquered fingers,
Kiss his mouth with summery lips, warmly tell him
Of my need for him and though my hopes have gone to seed
I need his love and believe in his gentle ways that ease all pain
So that in spite of everything I can rise up from this immense chasm
And stand on burning slabs, greeting the morning with a poem.

NA PIONNAÍ GRUAIGE

(Ó do chocáin dhonna
ó choillidh na gcnó, do dhuala raithní
is an raithneach ag ruadh)

Sa tseanbhabhla briste
caite sna driseoga ar chúl an tí
fód créafóige ina bhéal –

D'aimsigh mé sa tsalachar
na pionnaí gruaige a bhíodh ag mo mháthair
nuair a bhí mé beag.

San oíche an loinnir a bhíodh
ina ciabh chatach dhonn agus í ina bhun,
a chiaradh agus a scuabadh

Is ag cur na bpionnaí ann;
an ruaithne a thigeadh ó bhoinn óir a dlaíoga
faoi sholas an tilly

Eas copair a cuid gruaige
ag sileadh léithe, tuilidh dhrithlinneach
a cuid gruaige ag titim léithe.

A mhamaí, bhain do chuid gruaige
an buí de dhuilliúr an fhómhair, an boige
den tsíoda, an splanc den tsoilseach,

An sní de shruth na habhna.
Má b'é do chluasa mo dhá aingeal choimhdeachta
agus mé sa chliabhán, b'é

Do dhuala fada grástúla
méara Dé ag cur cigilt ionam sula dtéinn
chun suain gach oíche.

Má b'é do shúile glé
na toibreacha caoine as ar ól mé íc an ghrá,
b'é d'fholt craobhach

An crann a dhreap mé
chun na spéire, mo chosa i measc na bpláinéad,
mo cheann i bhfochair Dé.

I seanbhabhla briste
gach craic ann chomh caol le ribe
d'aimsigh mé sa tsalachar

Pionnaí gruaige mo mháthar;
pionnaí a théann go croí ionam is a folt
faoi chlár sa chaoineadh seo

HAIR PINS

(Your brown knots of hair,
These are hazel brown,
Your tresses bracken and the bracken reddening)

Among the remains
of a bowl cast among brambles –
the mouth of the bowl stuffed with earth

Here in the grime behind the house
I discovered hair pins
worn by my mother when I was small

At night her curly brown strands
shone as she tended her hair
combing and brushing

And putting in the pins;
single threads of gold
shining in the light of the tilly lamp

Her hair was a copper cascade
in free fall; a river of light
in full spate

Mammy, your hair stole
the yellow from autumn leaves, softness
from silk, the flash from lightning

The flow from the running stream.
If your ears were my guardian angels
as I lay in the cot,

Your long graceful locks
were God's fingers tickling me
every night before sleep.

If your glistening eyes were soft springs
from which I drank of your healing love,
your flowing head of hair

Was that forest I climbed
to reach the sky, straddling constellations,
my head resting in the bosom of God.

An old bowl
each crack as fine as a rib of hair
found among all the grime

And in it my mother's hair pins;
they needle me now
as her tresses mingle with the earth.

All three poems translated, from the Irish, by Gabriel Rosenstock.

Cathal Ó Searcaigh is the Irish Language Editor of this journal. His most recent volumes are Seal i Neipeal *(2004), a travelogue, and* Gúrú i gClúidíní *(2008), a collection of poems, both from Cló Iar-Chonnachta. His memoir,* Light on Distant Hills *(Simon and Schuster), is forthcoming in 2009.*

LANGUAGE, SHOES AND CAKES

Slavenka Drakulić

The space between.

March has already arrived, but in Berlin the snow is still falling. Falling in big flakes that cling to the hair and to the dry twigs of the row of rickettsial trees on the Ku'damm. Yet a day or two ago I heard the chirping of birds and thought that spring was here already. I think about Leipzig and the book fair.

This year I am going to Leipzig with two hats on: as a member of the jury that awards the prize "for European understanding" – the winner this year is Yuri Andrukhovych, the young Ukrainian writer – as well as a member of the delegation of writers from Croatia. Since I have never in my whole life been a member of a delegation, not even of the *Pioneers* [communist children's organisation], the role is completely foreign to me. All of a sudden, in the middle of this blizzard, I wonder how I had got into such a situation. What was I thinking of when I consented? Wasn't I being a bit rash, where had my political instinct gone at that moment, I wonder now, too late of course. Because there have been book fairs in Leipzig, Frankfurt and elsewhere in previous years, but no such invitations. Times change, though, and let's say that this is a little sign of this change – both that I was invited, and that I agreed. And anyway, at this very moment in Zagreb, Profil is publishing the second part of my collected works, and I can't any longer justify complaining about being cold-shouldered.

And, in fact, I have utterly no wish to deal with the political aspect of the whole story about representing or not-representing Croatia. I am interested in something completely other – language. My language, in which I write, in fact, my languages, and the space between them in which I sometimes happen to be. And unexpectedly I become aware that this space of not-belonging – in language and in life – is a bewildering but invaluable experience.

Last year, as winner of the very same prize for the book *They Would Never Hurt a Fly* I found myself in the same kind of situation. I had experienced such things earlier too, but this time it was brought closer home to me because of the official representatives of Croatia and Sweden.

After the announcement of the prize in January, in Berlin, the Swedish ambassador put on a reception in my honour, no great surprise, since I have Swedish as well as Croatian citizenship. And because Sweden thinks of me as a writer of its own, although not exactly its own, I would say, because I don't write in Swedish. But they are very decent and tolerant people. The Croatian ambassadress also wanted to put on a party for me, but since I was staying only a very short time in Berlin, it turned out that the two receptions were spontaneously held together, and we had the celebration in the residence of the Swedish ambassador, with the Croatian ambassadress and German and Croatian friends also attending.

Two months later, at the award ceremony in the Leipzig concert hall – the Gewandhaus Orchestra conducted by Herbert Blomstedt was playing – the same two ambassadors were among the invitees. Expressing my gratitude for the prize, I gave the speech in Croatian. And nothing here would have been very unusual except for a trifle that seemed to me rather paradoxical: the book for which I had won the prize was written in neither Croatian nor Swedish but in English.

A Croatian writer who doesn't write in Croatian? A writer who lives in Sweden but doesn't write in Swedish? And what is more, a writer who is not reckoned to belong to the anglophone area because she doesn't live in any of the countries in which the language is spoken or in any of the former colonies. Partially, if I am going to be really accurate, because English is not the language of my novels, but of my essays and journalism. Still, it amounts to a lot of writing and five books written in this language. Yet there was not a single ambassador of any country from the English language area there in the turnout, simply because the literatures of these languages do not count me among their writers. Geographical criteria for classification still prevail over and are stronger than linguistic .

And then, of course, I once again had this feeling of existing between, not so much the different countries in which I live (to which Austria ought to be added) but between the various languages. As if, at that moment, there on the stage, I had landed in no-man's-land. Perhaps more than ever, the fact that a good part of my work was hovering in a vacuum became clear to me. Marvellous, I said to myself, it's as if you are weightless, nothing is pulling you down, you have no obligations to anyone, you're free of context, of geography, politics and institutions. For you aren't anyone's, just your own. And I might almost have believed this had there not been a physical sensation of emptiness in the chest, like a hole that was expanding. As it had, long ago, when I left home, knowing I would never return.

I was 16. A few days earlier my father had said in a fury this unforgivable sentence, as it seemed to me then: Get out, get out of the house. It was a terrible sentence, one that I can still hear today, although I know that he did not mean it, and that he was sorry later. But my mother said nothing, she probably thought it would all soon blow over, this wasn't the first time he had been in conflict with his obstinate daughter. It was just his nature, hot-headed, an ordinary attack of temper that ought not to be taken seriously. But I did take it seriously, and left. And never went back.

I boarded a train for Zagreb. The train was standing at platform one of Rijeka Station, the compartment stank of cigarette ends, and the seats were upholstered in shabby brown vinyl. Outside, the dank autumn day was rubbing its nose up against the filthy window pane. This was supposed to be just a short visit to a girlfriend studying in Zagreb. While the train slowly clambered up the track towards Delnice, I knew that it was my final departure from home. I did not cry. And that was the first time I had the feeling of emptiness and dull pain, as if someone had hacked a lump of flesh off me. A feeling that I was not whole anymore.

Later on this feeling would occur from time to time, with every loss, every departure for ever, when friends went away and people close to me died. Suddenly even the country in which I had been born ceased to exist. I won't say it was the same kind of loss, but it was a loss, for a piece of my past had snapped off. Memories and the language remained, the last thing that you bid farewell to in your life. A lot can be made out of memories and language, and these two elements alone can be enough for writing, for the preservation of identity. And you can live off them for some time at least.

It happened, though, that with time the memories became less important than the present, that I gradually slipped out of the language, or that the language slid out of my life. Not the way that might be expected, the way Josef Brodsky describes, because my language was gradually becoming impoverished due to my not being in everyday contact with it, because it was melting like a snowball in the hand. No, I went out of (and went back to) my own language consciously, because a different language, English, allowed me a subsistence. And because it became the language of everyday communication. English became a parallel, "working", language for me. I set my borders: I would go on writing novels in my native language. Because for me it is the language of emotions, and in the novels it is with the emotions that I write.

And so a year ago in Leipzig I found myself between two countries and inside a third language. Is it possible to represent both one and the other? Should I choose? Why on earth was I asking myself this, had it suddenly become important to know where I belonged, was someone forcing me to make the choice? Perhaps I had become sentimental, like those old people beset by nostalgia, spending their lives on the docks or in the mines of South America, and who now, worn out, were coming back to their native island. It looks as if I am equating language and geography – but in fact it is to do language,perhaps to do with sentimentality about language. For at this moment, the geographical and political definitions are of minor importance. All of it is Europe, there are no borders between Sweden and Austria any longer, and even Croatia is on the way.

The language question is more important for me, because I know very well the difference between the two languages, the working language and the mother tongue: I get into one of them like new shoes that haven't yet been worn in, that I am conscious of the whole time I am walking. They are not tight, but not so entirely comfy that I can forget them. I put on the other like a pair of old slippers. I relax in this language. And I become increasingly conscious of its gravitational pull. It's not just about my attitude to the mother tongue being emotional, rather it is the language of my emotions, the trigger for my memories, and also for the physical sensation of emptiness, from time to time.

It is not possible to return to childhood and youth, I cannot resurrect my father or my brother, nor can I go back to a country that does not exist, and not even entirely to that in which I still live. And yet, it all exists, because it is a part of my present identity, composed of strata of the past and the present, of diverse countries and languages, friends and experiences. Like filo sheets in an apple strudel, like layers of creme in a torte. I feel this as the multiplicity of my identity, in which nothing is lost, nothing fades, one thing does not exclude another, they fit on top of each other, or alongside each other. Pain too is part of this, and the no-man's-land. Slipping away from the mother tongue sometimes does hurt, but entry into something else – into a new language, other milieu – is a gain. The hole gets filled up, the pain is assuaged, there is wholeness after all. I am here and there, included, present, counted in at least twice.

I thought about that last year when I was standing on the dais and speaking my text in my mother tongue.

And today, standing at the corner of the Ku'damm and Uhlanstrasse, while the snow is falling, I am thinking about slippers and cakes.

Translated, from the Croatian, by Graham McMaster.

One of her country's best-known writers, Slavenka Drakulić was born in Rijeka, Croatia, in the second Yugoslavia, in 1949. She studied comparative literature and sociology at the University of Zagreb, and worked as a journalist in the 1980s and early 1990s. She is the author of five works of fiction and five works of non-fiction, most recently in translation Café Europa: Life after Communism *(Penguin, 1996) and* They Would Never Hurt a Fly: War Criminals on Trial at The Hague *(Abacus, 2004). Owing to the threats she received due to her feminist and anti-jingoistic writings, she was forced in 1992 to emigrate from Croatia. She currently lives in Sweden and returns to the Balkans regularly.*

RETURN FROM EXILE

Bora Ćosić

Imbued with estrangement.

Now that most people are under the impression that a democracy of sorts has prevailed in Serbia, some people ask me if I will go back there, to my country, as if I had made a contract with my homeland with a lot of very precisely formulated provisions: a complicated document, verified before a court of law, which I and this state from my past have to observe; as if, should things take a turn for the better there, I should participate in this improvement. But as far as I recall, I signed nothing of the kind when I left. I just passsed by the young customs officers at the Kelebija border crossing, and they did not pay any particular attention to me. They had no inclination to see off a somewhat elderly gentleman in a grey suit. I think I was carrying one of my manuscripts then, and the rest of my possessions only arrived afterwards. Thus my exit from my homeland passed quite unnoticed and without any particular formalities. So no data exist on that event from our common history, that of my homeland and my own. Now there has been a change in this land in the south, whereas nothing has changed in the land of my body or the presidency of my soul. No coup has occurred in my being, and the rule of my reason still endures somehow.

Then I ought first to remember where, which space I would be returning to. Because when I left I took with me a part of that land, even though maybe a very tiny part indeed, so that there is nothing left there, where my former life used to be. That is why I believe that all this time I have been treading my own ground, only a part of which has moved over here. And the hospitable ground of my new land in the north parted a little so that it could accommodate a part of my former ground like an adjunct of sorts. This happens, anyway, in the course of dramatic tectonic shifts, entire mountains sliding away into the unknown and former valleys closing like the pages of an unread book. I believe, therefore, that such things may occur under circumstances that are quite peaceful, when a foreigner comes to a new environment, bringing with him, along with what has been packed in his suitcases, a tiny bit of his former country under his feet. And so I would never find that old space in the south, in that whole that used to be. And apart from this sample of my former ground, brought over along with the rest of the luggage, something very much like it has been brought over by other people, asylum seekers. So we who are here in the north could put together a sizeable piece of our homeland if we put our individual pieces of ground together, provided we cared to do so, that is. As for myself, however, I have been trying for years to join a part of my personal territory to the republic of the rest of the world, in the form of a private region of sorts. That is why I believe that my friends' hope for my return to the south is not realistic. For I no longer have that space where I used to be, just as I am unable to move back to that former time. A great predecessor of mine, the poet Crnjanski, also spent a quarter of a century in exile, and then made the mistake of returning to his former country, where most of his coevals were already dead, and the living regarded him as dead, with a host of honours and privileges also intended for the dead only. Thus I remember the great poet walking through the city of his past like a ghost. For no one can return to yesterday, let alone to a time a quarter of a century in the past. And then his former exile, walking through the city of his youth, appeared to have been exiled anew to some foreign land. For the place where he found himself then was the land of his senescence, senescence being like a special republic where he had arrived.

Thus I can no longer return to the space of my former life, the way that old Greek philosopher could not enter the same river twice. For the space of everyone's life is some kind of flow, whether a river or some other kind of flow, where everything appears to be on a sort of conveyor belt, a world exhibition of our fate. A lot of things are on display there in a very neat manner, making it easy to survey them; the only thing is, all these exhibits of being keep slipping away. One may therefore say that this former ground, even back then, while I still stood upon it, kept slipping away, as if both I and everything around me were on this conveyor belt. Human existence is just an exhibit on nature's market; we know not for whose eyes it is intended. It is possible that this huge fair of humankind has been made in order to amuse itself, irrespective of its surroundings. It is as if we are meant to buy ourselves at a reduced price while this exhibition lasts, and once the exhibition closes, everything will be much more expensive. That is my view of the ground I left behind, basically, except for some of its dust that stuck to my shoes. For human ground is mainly made of dust, only it gets more solid with time. That is another warning to excessive patriots who see the ground of their lives as a magical space. What they do not understand is that the ground of every people is a neutral substance that does not care much about those treading over it. All this trampling upon it may even get on its nerves. Hence I left that space of my past behind, thinking I got on its nerves occasionally by walking upon it, and I was nervous myself while walking upon it. My leaving, therefore, does not have political implications only. It may have been due to my nervousness, provoked by a number of things, not just that idiotic regime. All this is part of a discussion that I conduct with myself while listening to that question, put to me in a friendly tone, inquiring whether I would go back to my country. This is also what my friendly editor said to me here, in Zurich, opposite the café where Joyce used to sit, another exile from his own country who went into exile voluntarily. I believe that above all he ran away from his own family, from his father who maltreated his mother, from his mother who nagged at his father. And the remainder of the family just lingered on in that kitchen of Irish unease, and some very fine books emerged out of all this, arising, more often than not, from some kind of unease or other, not from anything in the way of an idyll. And this is why every man on the run should also be looked at from that angle, from the analytic perspective, so that we could see what sort of things bothered that person where he used to live and not just blame it all on some fool who happens to rule his stupid people just then. And as it turns out, in that abandoned space there was certainly some other reason to make one wish to escape, only there may not have been sufficient determination in that person's soul to do such a thing. One often finds oneself in a position of wishing to escape somewhere, anywhere, most of all from one's own skin. This being impossible, as the proverb says, there remains, at least, the possibility of simply changing places, if customs officials do not care very much when we show up at a border crossing, especially when we are a bit elderly and crossing that borderline in a grey suit, as if in some prize game. There is a lot of stuff of that kind in those silly TV competitions where a candidate is supposed to cross some line or other, or surmount an obstacle as quickly as possible. All those antics may be a reflection of the behaviour of people from these parts at border crossings. Instead of just showing their passports, they indulge in all sorts of silly movements and grimaces. All of the above is indicative of what thoughts course through my head when someone asks me, in a well-intentioned manner, whether I will go back to my former home, not taking into consideration at all what anyone's home may mean to one in a metaphysical sense as a metaphoric, a biological one perhaps. It is as if I were to return, once again, to the womb of my female parent.

Were I to return now to the place of my former life, I might feel as if I were inside a stage set. That is what everyone should probably feel anyway, that what one lives in is not something entirely "real", but that there is always something theatrical about it. So when a man returns after many years to the scene of life's crime, to him, that moment must feel as if he has just stepped from behind a curtain, for the performance is already finished. For whatever stands there looks like some human frame, while actually belonging to that part of our being imbued with estrangement. It is as if, aged nine, I walked out into the street after an illness and it was not that same old street. Now, due to my illness of exile, all that is only intensified. So I am unable to return to my former surroundings even if I wished to. The performance of my life there has finished, and as for myself, the only audience watching the performance of this play, I have gone out, gone home somewhere. For my current residence is the home everyone goes to after paying a visit to the theatre. And as for that which used to be the space of one half of my century, it is just a theatre, where a lot has been performed, only the lights have dimmed and nothing is being played any more. And so the places of my former residence await a new audience, which I am no longer a part of. So when I think of returning anywhere today, I dream of returning to my tranquillity of 10 years or so ago. And I can do that right here in my room in Charlottenburg.

Translated, from the Serbian, by Novica Petrović.

Bora Ćosić was born in Zagreb, Croatia, in the first Yugoslavia, in 1932. He studied philosophy at the University of Belgrade and edited a number of Yugoslav literary journals in the 1950s and 1960s. His voluminous and now-classic opus includes novels, short stories and journalism. In 1992, as a protest against the Milosevic regime, he left Serbia for Croatia and, subsequently, moved to Berlin, where he continues to live.

FRONTIERS

David Albahari

Message in a bottle.

1

I started thinking about frontiers in the early 1990s. Before that, I did not believe those who maintained that they existed.

2

In a society where many cultures are intertwined there can be no talk of frontiers. The existence of frontiers in a multicultural society actually means that the society in question is not a multicultural one, that within it one culture dominates, wishing to maintain its control over the other cultures. So far, I have not lived in such a society, a society of strictly controlled cultures. I grew up in one kind of multicultural society, the social-communist version that existed in the former Yugoslavia, and currently I live in its capitalist version in Canada. In fact, when the ideological layer is stripped away from both versions, one sees that there are no differences – a multicultural society either exists or does not exist; cultures either intertwine or languish, each in its own corner; artists either open up various influences or close themselves within the delimited space of their local tradition. And even though I am inclined to promote the values of a mixed culture, I must point out that I do not believe that it is in itself better than an independent, local culture. In both types of culture artists can produce valuable work; in both types of culture they can fall into the trap of ideological stereotypes; in both cultures they have to grapple with extracultural factors that seek to exert control over cultural trends. The only advantage of a multicultural society is that it makes it easier to confront the prejudices on which the policy of glorifying a mononational culture is based, even though that in itself is no guarantee that an individual originating from a mixed society will see through the mechanisms of prejudice that might direct him to the muddy dregs of racism.

3

Given that, for a long time, I did not believe in frontiers, I never felt that I was crossing them or that I was in the wrong territory. I perceived the mixed Jewish-Serb-Yugoslav culture that I grew up in as a whole, without any walls or doors, open to unrestricted movement, even when there were visible differences in those three segments. History, for example, plays a different part in them: Jewish tradition is based on a cyclical repetition of history; Serbian tradition glorifies history as defeat; Yugoslav tradition was based on a selective approach to history. The fact that I belonged simultaneously to all these traditions, however, did not force me to opt for one of them only but enabled me better to perceive the mechanisms functioning behind them and thereby see their drawbacks and advantages more precisely.

4

I am not speaking of identity here, for a choice of identity is not what, in the final analysis, defines a writer, unless I am very much mistaken. A writer is defined by his or her lanuage and style. Identity – understood as that which identifies the individual with the broader community that he or she belongs to – need not play any part in creation. A writer may feel, say, Serb or Jewish, without any of that feeling entering the prose or poetry that he or she writes. Kafka is a good example of this: if we say that he was a Jew writing in the German language in Prague, where does that place him? Is he a part of German literature, where he belongs on the basis of his choice of language, or Czech literature, where he belongs on the basis of his place of residence, or Jewish literature, where he belongs by origin? There are those who believe that it is precisely his style – reportedly based on the language of the Talmud – that determines him as a Jewish writer, even though there is nothing in his prose that would suggest a Jewish content. Others insist and that atmosphere of Prague is what makes Kafka Kafka, while the linguistic threads connecting him to German literature are the decisive factor for those who consider him to be a German writer. The best answer, perhaps, is that Kafka is all of the above, but also more than that: that he is actually a writer without frontiers, a multicultural writer in the best sense of the word, who transcends any limitation that may be imposed by identity, language or national tradition.

5

Naturally, no matter how we define them, frontiers tend to lead to a debate on affiliation, even in a situation when, for example, a writer attempts to live on the borderline, thus trying to avoid having to make any statements about belonging to one side or the other. Many, however, will not allow him or her to do this and will deny him or her the right to be what he or she wants. Literature, they say, is created out of a sense of affiliation, and that is the only thing that counts. And what about language? Is not language the only real affiliation of a writer, in view of the fact that the world he or she creates exists in language only and nowhere else? When, for example, Kundera writes in French, is he a Czech or a French writer? And when Skvorecky, who is a Canadian citizen, writes in Czech, is he an ethnic Canadian writer who survives owing to the policy of multiculturalism, or a Czech writer who does not want to go home any longer? These apparently different questions reflect the same situation: all these writers are in a fire-swept zone between different worlds, in borderline areas between languages, histories of literature and political systems. And they all survive precisely because they do not recognise frontiers.

6

Another thought occurs to me: that they all survive because their writing – maybe not in its entirety but certainly in parts – is a reflection of their yearning for what they are not, for what they could be if they recognised frontiers and then crossed them.

7

Naturally, frontiers are much more obvious when they are underlined by linguistic differences than when – as is usually the case with the Jewish community – such differences do not exist. For example, moving from a Jewish environment to a Serb one does not require a change of language, so that there is no real feeling of crossing from one "territory" to another. The language is the same on both "territories" and differences – for differences, whether we like it or not, will always exist – must be sought elsewhere.

8

We also find similar elements in writers who are forced – or have decided of their own accord – to live in exile. Again we have a crossbreeding of cultures and a possible conflict of languages, plus the fact that nostalgia plays an exceptionally significant role in the situation of an exile. A significant role is also played by political and ideological aspects, which often supress the issues that are decisive for literature, those of language, style and the mixing of cultures. In the final analysis, exile does not seem to be such a fearsome experience for writers, for irrespective of the popular myths of life in exile, most writers emerge victorious from their clash with the fate of an exile. The success of Isaac Bashevis Singer, Vladimir Nabokov, Joseph Brodsky, Czeslaw Milosz, Witold Gombrowicz and Julio Cortázar, for example, is incontrovertible proof of this.

9

Living in a multicultural society, then, may give a writer – or more precisely: a person who does not know yet that he or she will become a writer – the opportunity of gaining insight and understanding that could decisively influence his or her poetics. Such a life may also take him or her in quite the opposite direction: to becoming an advocate of frontiers, divisions and various kinds of spiritual and moral "purity", for the existence of a multicultural society need not automatically mean that the society in question has left behind all the negative aspect of cohabitation. The example of the former Yugoslav multicultural community shows precisely with what ease the positive characteristics of a multicultural society can turn into negative images and be abused for various political or nationalist ends. A Jew growing up in Serbia now, often confronted with expressions of open hatred towards Jews, will certainly develop a picture of multiculturalism quite different from that developed by other Jews who, like myself, grew up there in the 1950s and -60s, when things like that were very rare indeed. And while I, with my memories and owing to the fact that I now live far away, am ready to understand this and to justify it to a certain extent, a young Jew living in Serbia now probably increasingly doubts the possibility of a multicultural life and experiences the fears and anxieties that I was mercifully spared. Where I saw no frontiers he or she may see insurmountable walls.

10

The last 10 years or so, which I have spent far away from Zemun, have changed nothing in the picture I have sketched in the preceding passages.

One of the reasons for this certainly lies in the fact that in my new environment I have not tried to become a part of its literature and culture. Had I tried to do so, I do not doubt that – despite the official multiculturalism that is the norm here – I would have faced frontiers harder and harsher than those I occasionally encountered in my former environment. In point of fact, these frontiers would be what I am inclined to call guild boundaries,warnings not to enter the territory of others, warnings that – especially since I do not write either of the official languages – I am an intruder after all, but frontiers are frontiers, and no matter where they originate, they create a feeling of sickness in me. That is why I have elected to play the role of an uninterested guest, which gives me freedom of movement through another culture without coming into conflict with those already living there. Thus my original cultural region remained unchanged, even though I am there more often in my dreams and reveries than in reality. It is this distance, however, that has enabled me to see to what extent I am indebted to the Yugoslav mixture of cultures I grew up in, especially the interplay of Serbian and Jewish culture. In view of the fact that this mixture no longer exists, and that I refuse to give it up, it is no wonder that I feel like a shipwrecked person to whom no land appears safe enough. I sit on a raft and send messages in bottles. The sea is sometimes stormy, sometimes calm, never quite dependable, but one thing is certain: it never recognises frontiers.

A novelist, short-story writer and translator, David Albahari was born in Peć, Serbia, in the second Yugoslavia, in 1948. He is the author of eight novels and eight collections of short stories, as well as a translator of a number of works from English into Serbian. In 1994, he moved with his family to Calgary, Canada, where he still lives.

LORCA'S SLEEPWALKING BALLAD

Máire Mhac an tSaoi

Arna aistriú ó Spáinnis Gipsy Ballads.

SPAISTE AN CHOLLATÁNAIGH

'Ghlasuaine, is tú mo ghrá!
'Ghlasuaine is tusa 'charaimse!
Glasuaine iad gaoth agus craocha …
Ar bord na loinge ar muir
I muinín an eich ar na hardaibh
D'rochadas is guirtéal di,
Ag taibhreamh di ar lochta in airde
Glasuaine a lí 's a cúl gruaige.
'S a fuarshúil mar airgead raolach.
'Ghlasuaine, is tú mo ghrá
Fé sholas ghealach na nÉigipteach,
Gach ní ag faire uirthi-se,
Is ní fhaireann sise iad chuici.

'Ghlasuaine, is tú mo ghrá!
Realanna móra reoite,
Le hiasc na scamall ag snámh dóibh,
Ar leathadh de chonair na maidne;
Ceann fíge ag cimilt na gaoithe
Le raspa líofa duilliúrach,
Is an cnoc, gramhasach mar chat,
Ag beartú ingne faoir di.
Ach cé thagann? Cad as a dtagann?
Ise fós ar an lochta in airde…
Glasuaine a lí ' s a cúl gruaige
Ag taibhreamh di ar ghoirteamas mara.

"Úncail, á malartóinn
Mo chapall anso ar do thig-se?
An iallait ar do scáthán?
Is mo scian á thabhairt ar do chóta?
Úncail, táim tagtha ag cur fola
Ó d'fhágas dóirse na Ceábrach,"
"Á mba ar mo chumas é, a dhalta,
Do bheadh an méid sin 'na mhargadh,
Ach feasta ní mise mé féin,
Ná mo ghnáthóg thí ní líom féin é."
"Úncail dá mb'fhéidir mo mhian
Sheathlóinn go macánta ar chnaiste
Mo leapan ar cholpaí iarainn,
Fé bhairlíntí den lín Olóinteach.
Féach mar ropadh mo chliabhrach
Ón imleacán 'dtí an bhrád orm!"
"Trí chéad de rósanna cradhracha
Bláthaíonn i mborlach do léin,
Tuileann an fhuil fád' chrios,
Is éiríonn uait blath na fola …
Ach fós ní mise mé féin
Is mo ghnáthóg thí ní liom féin é!"
"Ceadaigh dom ar a laíod
Dreapadh chun an lochta in airde
Ceadaigh dom dreapadh in airde
Mar a bhfuil an lochta glasuaine,
Lochta, fé sholas na ré,
A sileann an t-uisce anuas uaidh."

Suas leo, an bheirt úd mhuinteartha,
Suas chun an lochta in airde,
Lorg na fola 'na ndiaidh
Is lorg na ndeor anuas air.
Tóirsí ar shligí den stán,
Criothann ar fuaid na ndíon slinne,
Míle bodhrán den gcriostal,
Goineann siad lóchtaint na maidne.

'Ghlasuaine, is tú mo ghrá,
Is tusa 'charaimse 'Ghlasuaine ...
Dreapann an bheirt chompánach.
Leanann leithead na gaoithe
Mar bhlas ina mbéal ón alltar,
Mar a bheadh blas den domlas,
Den mhismín is den triúr drifearach ...
"'Úncail, abair cá bhfuil sí?
Cá bhfuil iníon sin an léin uait?"
"Fada dhi ag fanúint leat!
Ró-fhada fós is ea fhanfaidh!"
Snó is úire, folt is ciardhubha,
Glasuaine an lochta mar 'fhanann ...

Ó scáil na haghaidhe ins an umar,
Scanraíonn an cailín Éigipteach ...
Glasuaine a lí 's an cúl gruaige,
Fuarshúile mar airgead raolach,
Ar shnáthad oighre ón ngealaigh
Ag snámh dóibh ar bharr an uisce ...
D'iompaigh an oíche 'na rún
Mar fhaiche bheag i mbaile iargcúlta.

Buaileann gardaí an stáit
Ar meisce dhóibh ar an ndoras ...
'Ghlasuaine, is tú mo ghrá!
'Ghlasuaine, is tusa 'charaimse!
Ar bord na loinge ar muir
'S i muinín an eich ar na hardaibh!

Do Cathal Ó Searcaigh

"The Sleepwalking Ballad" is one of 15 celebrated poems by Frederico Garcia Lorca, written between 1924-27, which he titled Gipsy Ballads *(*Romancero Gitano). *They explore,* inter alia,*various forms of sexuality, combining the ballad's tradtional narrative form with startling, allusive and surreal imagery. Here a wounded gipsy smuggler, sought by the Civil Guard, returns to the house of his beloved. An English translation of the poem can be found in Michael Hartnett's* Gipsy Ballads *(Goldsmith Press, 1974).*

One of the past century's most important Irish language writers, Máire Mhac an tSaoi was born in 1922 and educated at University College Dublin and the Sorbonne. Her first collection of poems, Margadh na Saoire *(Sáirséal & Dill) was published in 1956; her most recent,* Shoa agus Dánta Eile *(Sáirséal Ó Marcaigh), in 1999. Her acclaimed memoir,* The Same Age as the State *(O'Brien Press), appeared in 2003. She is married to Conor Cruise O'Brien and lives in Howth, Co Dublin.*

POEM

Elaine Gaston

EVEN ON SUNDAYS

for Kathryn

Even on Sundays
in the middle of the summer
we had to wait
on our farm
through the heat of the day,
find the cool of long grasses
the shade of sycamore trees,
dreams of ice-cream cones, sand
and other children
at the seaside,
wait

until after the pigs were fed,
nine o'clock in the evening
and then

only then
did we pack the car up
take our togs
and slip off
when the moon was rising
sky still bright
sun still up

to Tyrella Beach or somewhere near
only ten miles in the car
the County Down countryside
changing from cow parsley and hawthorn
to marram grass, drumlin and sand dune

the beach deserted,
sea still and calm
no wind
the end of the day

then
and only then
did we slip into peaceful water
warming as it rose
onto the day's hot sand,

moon full
tide high.

Elaine Gaston was born and raised in Co Antrim, and attended Oxford University. Her poems have appeared in The Word of Mouth Anthology *(Blackstaff Press, 1996), as well as a number of Irish and British journals.*

PORTFOLIO

Fifteen Photographers

Marine Micrographs.

Sergestes larva
(deep-water decapod crustacean: 30x)

Solvin Zankl
Kiel, Germany

These photographs of marine life are among the winning entries over the last three years in the Nikon SmallWorld Photomicrography Competition, whose aim is to showcase the beauty and complexity of life and matter as seen through the light microscope. Since 1974, the Competition has recognized the excellence and proficiency of scientific photomicrographers engaged in research in the life sciences, materials science and bio-research. Any specimen or subject, and all varieties of light microscopy, are eligible. Details of the annual competition can be found at www.nikonsmallworld.com. All micrographs are published courtesy of Nikon SmallWorld.

The Editors wish to thank Beth Starkin of Peppercom Communications in New York City for her assistance in assembling this selection of micrographs.

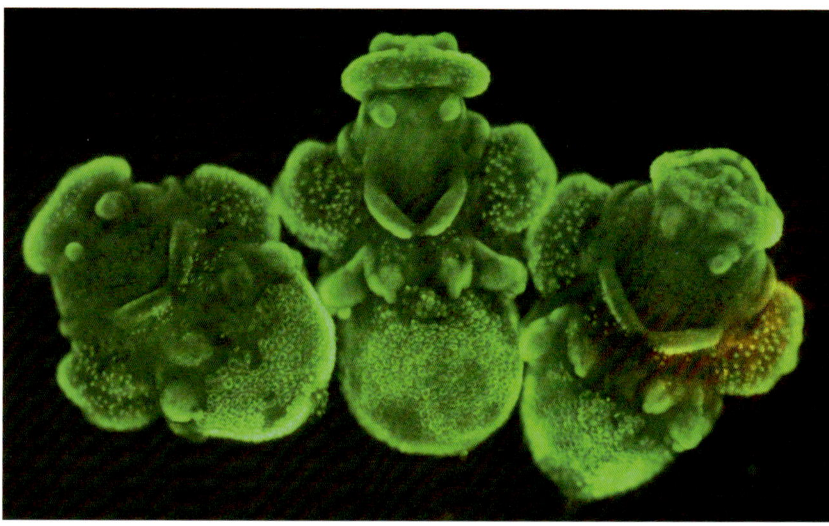

Loligo pealei
(squid embryos at five days: 80x)

Rachel Fink
South Hadley, Massachusetts, United States

Diatoms on red alga
(100x)

Wim van Egmond
Rotterdam, Holland

Live marine polychaete worm
(fireworm: 40x)

Jasper Nance
Moscow, Idaho, United States

Cynobacteria
(20x)

Jose Almodovar
Mayaguez, Puerto Rico

Coiled radula of *Patella vulgaris*
(mollusc: 20x)

Stephen Lowry
Coleraine, Northern Ireland

Homarus americanus larvae
(American lobster: 40x)

Alistair Dove
Stony Brook, New York, United States

Atlanta peronii
(gastropod mollusc: 170x)

Peter Parks
Witney, England

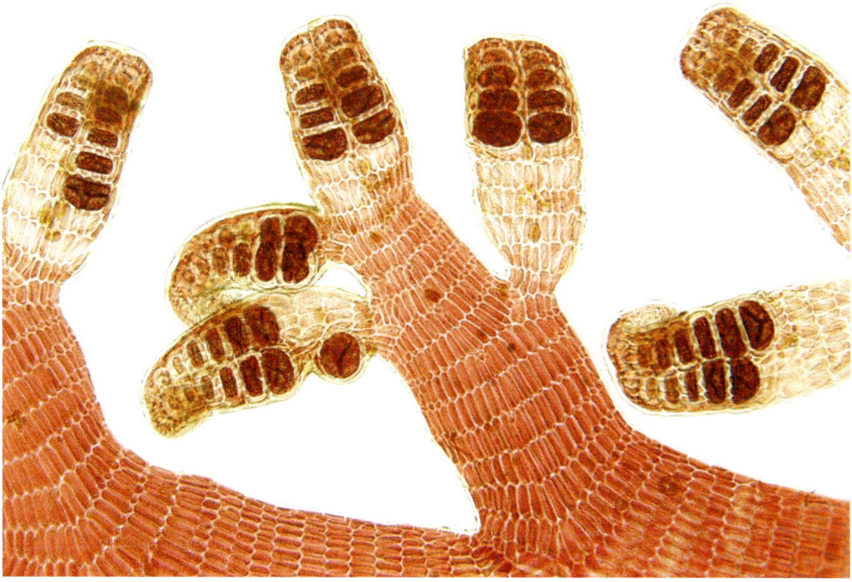

Amansia
(red seaweed reproductive branches: 100x)

John Huisman
Murdoch, Western Australia

Diatoms
(100x)

Jose Almodovar
Mayaguez, Puerto Rico

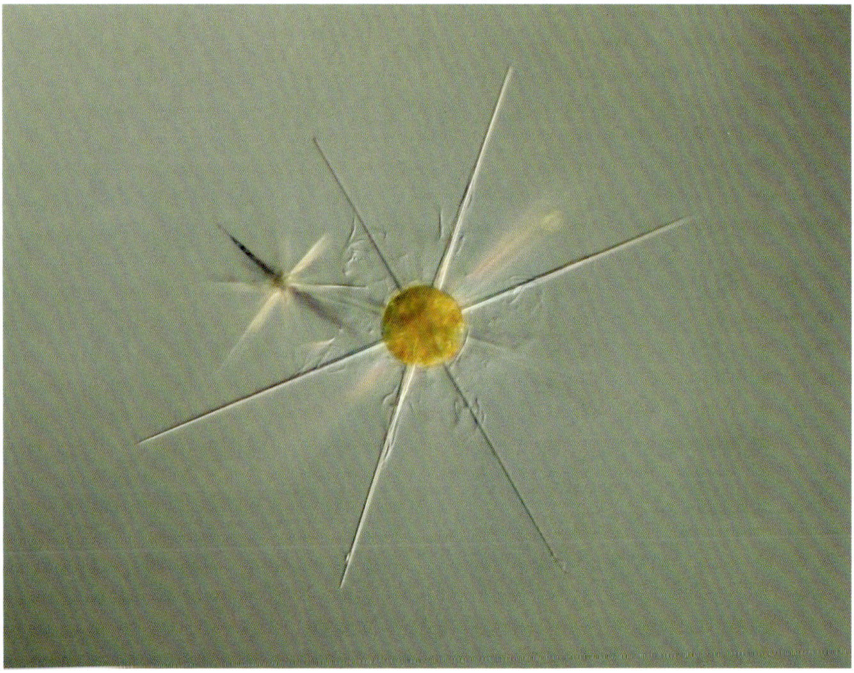

Living radiolarium
(20x)

Bernd Walz
Golm, Germany

Hypomyzostoma on a crinoid echinoderm
(50x)

Greg Rouse
La Jolla, California, United States

Hydractinia uniformis
(66x)

Sérgio Stampar
Sao Paulo, Brazil

Pleurosigma
(marine diatoms)

Michael Stringer
Westcliff, Essex, England

Clione sp. larva
(planktonic mollusc: 40x)

Mathew Hodge
Portland, Oregon, United States

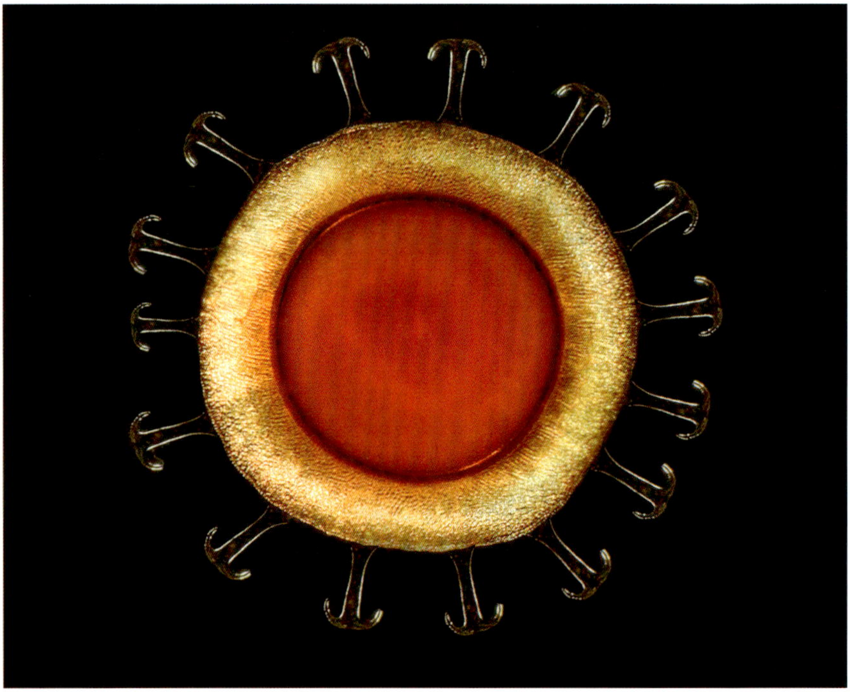

Bryozoan statoblast
(aquatic animal of the phylum Bryozoa: 10x)

Chiedozie Ukachukwu
Rodchester, New York, United States

PORTFOLIO
is generously supported by Nicholson & Bass Ltd, Belfast.

PROSE AND TWO POEMS

Peter Sirr

THIS IS NOT AN EDITORIAL

Gatecrashing the poetry party.

Hard to believe I've handed in my fifteenth issue of *Poetry Ireland Review*. How did that happen? The initial idea was to do eight issues as the organisation felt that the *Review*, at this stage of its journey, would benefit from a longer span of editorship. Eight turned to 12 and then I was asked to hold the fort for another three issues as PI went through some changes of its own, and, all pleas for mercy having fallen on deaf ears, this I agreed to do.

Now that it's over, what will I miss? Editing a magazine is a strange business, hard to quantify, or even to describe exactly. The activity itself lies somewhere between sloth and panic, and between intent and happenstance. Vague ideas slide around the back of the mind, poets who might be encouraged to submit, themes that might be tackled, writers that might be prevailed upon to deliver a think-piece. What about Wales? Afghanistan? What about Mangan, MacNeice, Mandelstam? Some things are there to be dealt with: the massive pile of submissions, for one. For many editors this is the most daunting aspect of the job. A magazine like *PIR*, with its national and international remit, attracts a dizzying volume of submissions. Many of these are what I'd call routine despatches – little bundles fired off to every journal that appears on a list, where the poet rarely bothers to read the journal and get a sense of what might be acceptable. Most of the submissions are not publishable – they're just not interesting enough, not well-enough written. Reading them can be a dispiriting chore. And yet there are the real finds, bright poems by unfamiliar writers, good work by established ones, and the small pile of definites begins to grow. You cheer up.

You quickly realise that very many good poets, particularly Irish poets, don't submit work. You also realise that many poems are well-enough written to be publishable – and yet they don't excite. They do not cause the hair on the back of the neck to stand up. The editorial heart doesn't stop, nor breath shorten. Their language is inert, the subjects are boring. Poets can often seem to be working a narrow little seam of private experience. They don't seem to get out much. This seems to be particularly the case with poetry in English. An enormous variety of poetry of every possible hue is written in English but only a particular strain of it ends up, for the most part, on the *PIR* desk. The editor in search of poetic adventure has to labour a little to find it.

PIR is an Irish magazine, but I didn't take that to mean a magazine of Irish poetry. It's true that there is a serious effort to assess Irish-published work and to feature work by Irish poets, and these are both built into the fabric of the *Review*. But – and here comes some good old bias – a large part of me thinks that the whole notion of Irish poetry is fairly boring, a kind of branding exercise for a product few, if put to it, could really define. The currents of poetic influence flow across continents and languages and few poets would seek to confine themselves within national boundaries, or to measure themselves against a set of "national" criteria. The dismaying parochiality of so much of Irish critical and cultural discourse – not least the flawed concept of "Irish Studies" – shouldn't blind us to the internationalism that is the lifeblood of poetry. Those who assume the exceptionality of Irish poetry will witter on about the lines of influence from Yeats to Heaney to Muldoon and ignore the fact that Montale, Pessoa, Celan, Bonnefoy, Lowell, Murray and a host of other unacknowledged legislators have long since gatecrashed the party. I put a lot of poems in translation into the *Review* not least because a good part of my everyday reading consists of exactly that, and a magazine may as well be as attentive to the idle browsing of its editor as to his, em, considered interventions. But I actually don't know any serious practitioners who don't have an ear cocked to the news from elsewhere, and aren't excited by what they discover from one end of the planet to the other. We're at home in our language and necessarily imprisoned in our own little context, but the spices we cook with are as likely to be imported as home-grown.

"Have you no funny stories to entertain us?" "Editing is an exciting and dangerous business, isn't it?" "Did you never get a clatter on the ears or a box on the jaw for your pains?" True enough, if you haven't made enough enemies in life, then you need a spell in an editor's chair to set the balance right. The stock in trade of editing is disappointment. Back in the eighties we paid doleful visits to what we called the Careers and Disappointments

Officer to contemplate the bleakness of our futures, and being an editor is a bit like that in that most of those who knock on the door are not going to walk out smiling. I often had to say no to good work because there simply wasn't room for it, and found very little pleasure in the god-like decision-making aspect of the job. You're aware of how idiosyncratic personal taste is – and yet your job is to trust your own instincts and not let too much else get in the way. You need to believe that the final result is important: a magazine that can stand on its feet and not be hobbled by platitude, cosiness or corporatism. And then you need to go away and have a drink and forget about it.

I was lucky to have in the background an organisation and individuals fanatic in their devotion to the persistence of this journal, and an assistant editor, Paul Lenehan, whose eye for detail far exceeded mine, and I was equally blessed to have a range of contributors prepared to risk sending poems and to sit up late perfecting reviews and essays. The survival for more than a year of any literary outlet is miraculous, and maybe it's only professional organisations that can sustain the effort indefinitely. For me it's great to be able to go and to know *PIR* will continue to drop through the letterbox every three months. The editor is dead. Long live the editor.

This article first appeared in Poetry Ireland News, *the bi-monthly newsletter of Poetry Ireland. Poetry Ireland/Éigse Éireann is the national organisation for poetry in Ireland, serving all 32 counties and publishing* Poetry Ireland Review. *(Poetry Ireland, 2 Proud's Lane, Dublin 2 / T: 01 478 9974 / Email: poetry@iol.ie / Website: www.poetryireland.ie)*

TWO POEMS

Vital or virtual?

THE DIFFERENT RAINS COME DOWN

For motto the darting snipe
the curlew, the tree house
to which every morning I climb
bearing with aplomb
a flask of coffee, last night's line.

*

Deep in the hut the silence
roots. Days here. How long?
The meadow sings all day.
Reed-song, the lake spreads its music.

*

Yesterday
travelling though the country again
in the old jalopy, down the little roads
with only the graveyards signed
the dead handing us on
from townland to townland
until we found the junction

*

I lift the binoculars, move for a field
the sun has fallen on, has
fallen for, and soaked with light

in the middle a tree
like everyone's memory

*

Mist this morning
the hedges webbed with dew.

*

September breakfast:
a mouthful of blackberries in the lane.

*

I lift the binoculars: intimacies
of trees and cattle

sudden drift of smoke
sudden flitting on a wire
sudden roof
bats, suddenly,
like too fast films

suddenscape

*

Crex crex
in the callows
the corncrake survives
to be counted by the Corncrake Officer
is it not all
I could ever have wanted

*

The lake lies half hidden
at the end of the meadow, sending out
its reed legions
to sway drunkenly as they struggle
with the burden of the water

*

On the days he's not there
I tramp to my friend's house on the hill
and make coffee in his kitchen, I drink
from his mug, look out from his window
down towards the grey splash of the lake.
Still there, my mute swans, my life!
My friend sweats in the city
or has crept into my hut to drink from my mug
and train my binoculars on the gap between the trees
into his own distant life

*

The different rains come down
differently orchestrated
configurations of the rain
on corrugated iron
winter music, summer song
small surprise
of the secondary rain of trees
an after rain
bestowed like a gift
as you enter the canopy

*

Whatever you were
you scared the dog
and made him whimper

welcome or warning
your eyes shone
at the edge of the light

and the signs were all there
that absolute dark
the sound you made

as you ran down the road
almost colliding with us
before slipping into the field

or you were nothing
neither curse nor blessing
you were

yourself purely, your eyes blazing
caught in the porch glow
where you circled behind us

to take us in. Cold-eyed
briefly curious
and quickly gone

you left behind
a living dark, the black road
suddenly crowded

and the night filling like a corridor
all of us are passing through
with hardly a breath

between us. . .

*

Standing outside in the evening quiet
avid for light, for how the trees collect it,
disburse it, how the lower branches shine
with a colour combed out of the lake
and washed with reeds

listening to the sound a place makes
flittings and undersongs stitched into the air,
the creaturely silence, things
shifting and loosening,
a wren now from the eaves

darting to grass, then hesitating back;
standing at the edge of it as if to inhabit
some part of the conversation,
but just the way a hesitation inhabits a language,
no wren codes, deciphered trees

but standing there like nothing at all,
a post brushed by moth-wings,
a stillness rent with little cries,
a body thinned to bone like a hook
the mind might throw its hat on and forget.

SHHH

[shhh]

The counter intelligence community registers its disquiet
too many of us now, too much getting out

it's an awkward day for dentists as the case drags on
and no one much is smiling now, not the firemen

nor the baggage handlers, nurses, first time buyers
and since they changed the city boundaries and lowered the fares

my taxi driver's blue with rage, who never asked anyone to live in
Celbridge
or fucking Maynooth, but what it must be to sit back in the evening

with your tooth repaired and your bags intact, watching
the last of the light revive the carpet and know

you've passed your five yearly vetting review, your grandparents
haven't let you down, your teenage son, your childhood friend

haven't spilled the beans, no one has marched from the grave
to rattle his bones and bloody the carpet, and you are whole again

a re-trusted member of the counter intelligence community
your swipe card unlocks the canteen again, knowledge swamps the room

and you can cross the boundaries with your ear to the ground
your eyes on the cockpit, your whole body

as long as it lasts pressed to the pulse of the unquiet planet. Shhh!

*

[electricity speaks]

Electricity speaks your language, no translation necessary
everybody is afraid of electricity, and rightfully so

Nova Products says: it's possible to use anything for torture
but it's a little easier to use our devices

and someone sits quietly in an office high above the traffic
filling in the requisition order: three black, four white, three pearl

software tracks the invoices, the multilingual client feedback forms
proofread at an excellent rate and posted on the site

*

[the new regime inherits the electrodes]

Software lives and is replicated, it's a code re-use
the new regime inherits the electrodes

and it's a long day with a busy agenda
tunable munitions, psychotronics, voice to skull technologies

coffee in a foam cup and networking in the information hall
Electronic Intelligence offers The House of Fun torture chamber

here on the border the algorithms multiply, where peace
is not always human and not always lethal

self-deciding sentinels clean out the zone
denying access, keeping costs down

*

[old]

Software registers the schoolgirl
taken to the Railway Square at dawn
where the judge stands impatient, the noose in his hands

today's small story
heaped outside the morgue
green cords around the necks, the bodies drilled with holes

old enough to die
in a hail of bombs in the ancient city
who clamber up the bulletins now

and fall back
to the quenched playgrounds
and the silence of the search engines

*

[for the hanged boys]

For the hanged boys
what? An eternity unviolated

that they walk together
through the alleys of paradise

that they lie down
in the name of nothing but themselves

that they lie unwatched, untouched
their bodies restored

as the unreachable cities
fade and fall, the squares

silent and the cranes
disassembled, the applauding hands

disassembled, bone, dust, in the name
of nothing scattered to the winds.

*

[a dream]

Software conceals the electrodes, relentless
engines trawl the planet but the truth
is post-processed and harmless. Here
the vanished maps, the stalled tanks and the dead
returned, here the eternally inviolate
harvest and harvesters, the voices soft in the dusk.

Peter Sirr was born in Waterford in 1960 and educated at Trinity College, Dublin.He has published seven collections of poems with Gallery Press, most recently Selected Poems *(2004) and* Nonetheless *(2004). A new collection,* The Thing Is, *will be published by Gallery in 2009.*

POEM

Michael Longley

VISITING STANLEY KUNITZ

I have flown the Atlantic
To reach you in your chair.
Cuddling up, we talk about
Flowers, important things,
And hold hands to celebrate
Spring gentian's heavenly
(Strictly speaking) blue.
You grow anemones,
You say, wind's daughters.
I say the world should name
A flower after you, Stanley.
We read each other poems.
You who'll be a hundred soon
Take forever to sign
My copy of *Passing Through*.
What flower can I offer you
From Ireland? Bog asphodel
Is the colour of your shirt.
Grass of Parnassus? Mountain
Everlasting in New York?
Your zimmer-gavotte suggests
Madder with its goose-grassy
Tenacity, your age-spots
Winter-flowering mudwort.
But no, no. Let it be
Spring gentian, summer sky
At sunset, Athene's eyes,
Five petals, earthbound star.

Professor Michael Longley is the current holder of the Ireland Chair of Poetry. The rotating three-year Chair was established by the Arts Councils of Southern and Northern Ireland, Trinity College, Dublin, Queen's University Belfast, and University College, Dublin, to recognize the exceptional achievement of Irish poets in world literature. His most recent volume of poetry is Collected Poems *(Cape, 2006). He lives in Belfast.*

HISTORY OF BELFAST

Patricia Craig

Benn's civic masterpiece.

Come all ye dry-land sailors and listen to my son
'Tis only forty verses so I won't detain yis long.

The opening lines of the famous Belfast song "The Cruise of the Calabar" were probably not known to George Benn – I doubt if the song was current in his day – but certainly he was familiar with every view of Belfast and every detail of Belfast life in the period he set out to document: that is, from the earliest times to the opening years of the nineteenth century. Taking a cue from "The Calabar" I don't intend to detain yis long here, though Benn's monumental history is certainly equivalent to the forty verses specified, and more. It is also, as Jonathan Bardon has put it, indispensable: "One of the most impressive local histories written in the nineteenth century". Indeed, virtually every commentator on any aspect of Belfast's history has paid tribute to the invaluable and indefatigable Benn. Robert Johnstone, for instance, refers in one of his books to "George Benn's great work . . . the three-inch-thick door-stopper of a tome he laboured for a lifetime to produce". Ciaran Carson opens his "Question Time", in *Belfast Confetti*, by quoting Benn. And even D.J. Owen, whose own *History of Belfast*, published in 1921, is sometimes referred to as the book people have to make do with when they can't get hold of a copy of the Benn – even he declares himself to be "indebted" to his great predecessor "for a good deal of our knowledge of the early history of the town".

Who was George Benn? A biographical note at the back of Owen's *History* gives us a few of the facts. Benn was born in Tandragee in 1801 but grew up in Belfast from the age of eight and was educated, like many another literary luminary of the nineteenth century, at Inst – where we stand at this moment. He was only 22 when his first *History of Belfast* was published in 1823; but his more exhaustive masterwork took him another forty-odd years to complete. It came out in 1877 and was followed three years later by a supplementary volume taking us up to the year 1810 (published just two years before Benn's death in 1882). It was truly a lifetime's work, and it was helped by a collection of manuscripts amassed by a William Pinkerton which felicitously came into Benn's possession. Pinkerton had intended to write a history of Belfast himself, but he never got around to it – and we should be grateful that the task eventually fell to George Benn, who brings not only a scholarly inquisitiveness and density, but an occasionally idiosyncratic informality to bear on the subject.

You have to give him full marks for comprehensiveness, but he makes it clear, for instance, that he isn't riveted by statistics relating to the water supply of Belfast in 1678, though dutifulness obliges him to put these in. What's more to his liking is the occasional intriguing snippet such as the report concerning a respectable bookseller from North Street, and a Chaplain of the American Navy, who were found lying dead drunk in Rosemary Street in 1816 – and this in the vicinity of Roger Mulholland's beautiful elliptical church to boot, no doubt causing affront to a lot of Belfast Presbyterians going about their religious duties. "Why the bookseller allowed himself to be overcome in Rosemary Street with the American Chaplain", says Benn, "is rather inexplicable." And, when he comes to the topic of "Literary Persons of Belfast of the Eighteenth Century", he's forced to conclude that "it is unsatisfactory to mention that this branch of the subject is much more scanty than could be wished for". It would be pleasant to envisage George Benn sitting on a cloud somewhere in the stratosphere and observing the vast improvement in this area that has come about in the century and more since his death.

The first part of Benn's *History of Belfast* is exactly what it says, a general history, more or less beginning with the Elizabethan era, when Belfast consisted of nothing more than "a solitary castle among the desolate wastes". It grew slowly and was not for some time considered very desirable as a place of residence – even as late as 1690, Benn tells us, Belfast did not rank very high as a "healthful" spot, and King William of Orange was urged not to linger in it in case he might catch some indigenous infection. He had lately come from Carrickfergus where, according to one report, a chair was brought to the quayside on which the king sat down for a long rest before mustering his forces and dashing off to the Boyne, taking in Belfast along the way. (The chair was supposed to have found its way to St George's Church in Belfast, where for all I know it still is.)

Chapter Eleven moves on from general to social history with the Old

Town Book of Belfast – the seventeenth-century records. This section also includes an ecclesiastical history of Belfast, which I have to say I have not read with due care and attention. More to my taste is the "Description of the Old Streets of Belfast", though I'm nearly driven to tearing my hair when I read about "the fine old houses which run from Castle Place to Fountain Street", not to mention the Old White Linen Hall with its pleasant walks and shady groves. Alas, all these were destined for annihilation – "the ruthless builder", Benn says, "was preparing to mar all these beauties" – including the beauties of Peter's Hill, distinguished in the distant past for its gardens and orchards. Architectural outrage is not a phenomenon of the present; it simply changes its focus with the particular destructiveness inflicted on every generation.

Even if it's hard now to imagine grazing herds in Bedford Street, or women gathering violets in Ye Fields beyond Sandy Row in the 1680s, it's wonderful to have, in a reasonably compact form, the means to conjure up such fragments of bygone Belfast, along with all its complexities of ancient and modern history. This unique and enticing book has long been unavailable, except to scholars browsing in the recesses of libraries, or mad collectors with unlimited funds; and it is immensely to the credit of Belfast City Council and Blackstaff Press that it is once again in circulation among the general public. With its wealth of detail, its scholarly expertise, its readability, and its value to local and general historians, it is something that no home should be without – certainly no Belfast home. I'm sure that all of you can't wait to get your hands on a copy, if you haven't already done so, so I'll stop here.

These remarks were delivered at the launch of a facsimile edition of George Benn's A History of the Town of Belfast *(Blackstaff Press, 2008) at the Royal Belfast Academical Institution ("Inst") on 21 October 2008.*

A critic, anthologist and non-fiction writer, Patricia Craig was born in Belfast and lived for many years in London. Her most recent books are The Ulster Anthology *(2006) and* Asking for Trouble *(2008), both from Blackstaff Press. She now lives in Antrim with her husband, the painter and wood-engraver Jeffrey Morgan.*

DAVID PARK

Glenn Patterson

I don't know how many of you have travelled here this evening from East Belfast, but any of you who have will perhaps have seen one of the great Belfast sights, the starlings flocking above the Lagan around the Albert Bridge: "great shifting parabolas... shading the sky in charcoal", as they appear on p.22 of *The Truth Commissioner.*

I don't know either how many of you are regular listeners to Radio Ulster's *Good Morning Ulster*, nor indeed if there is any correlation between listening to it and living east of the Lagan, but if you did happen to be tuned in about two Monday mornings ago, you may have heard an explanation for the geometrical precision of those parabolas.

It seems that every single starling has at any given moment seven other starlings in its field of vision. As they move, so it moves.

It struck me listening to this that this was in some way analogous with the feat achieved by David Park not just on p.22 of *The Truth Commissioner*, but from p.1 to p.372.

The novel, for any of you who have not read it, or heard the Radio 4 serialisation, or seen the growing number of ecstatic reviews, interweaves the stories of four main characters – Henry Stanfield, Francis Gilroy, James Fenton, and Danny, aka Michael Madden – bringing them inexorably to a narrative union in the old Harland and Wolff Drawing Office, transformed for the purposes of the novel into the venue for Northern Ireland's own Truth and Reconciliation Commission.

It is a feat of empathy as well as choreography, of novelist's craft allied to an attentive citizen's ear.

I say it interweaves the stories of four main characters, but there is a fifth character, whose presence in the book is all the more marked by virtue of his absence from the lives of those who loved him. It is not to give anything away, or at least anything that you will not pick up in the first half dozen pages, to tell you that Conor Walshe has been the victim of an IRA murder and that at the heart of this novel is the vexed question – it's Northern Ireland, we only do *vexed* questions – of how we deal with the past.

I first read the novel in proofs late last summer. I remember being impressed by David's bravery – some would call it foolhardiness – in setting something if not today exactly then certainly no later than the day after tomorrow.

Wasn't there a possibility that the novel would be overtaken by – outdated by – events.

At the time of its actual writing there was no guarantee that the Stormont Executive would ever be up again, or once up able to do more than stagger a few steps before collapsing once and for all.

And as for a Truth and Reconciliation Commission, well it seemed to come in and out of fashion as often as, I don't know, straight-legged jeans. (What, are they out again?)

Of course the success of this novel does not depend on the accuracy of its predictions. Still in the circumstances it is remarkable how much David Park has got right. He even had the foresight to create a cameo for the driver of his prominent Sinn Féin politician.

We still do not, it is true, have a Truth Commissioner, although we do, as of the end of last month, have not one but four new Victims' Commissioners, or one for every twenty-seven members of our overcrowded Assembly. As for whether we will ever have the equivalent of Henry Stanfield (the equivalent of his office, I mean, not, God hopes, his character), or whether indeed we need, or could cope with such an office, that is something on which you will all no doubt have your opinion.

All I will say is that in doing what art has always done, creating the one that stands for the many, David Park's novel deals as eloquently and movingly with the past in its 372 pages as any government instituted body could in many, many millions more.

Northern Ireland might never have a Truth Commission, but it is very, very fortunate indeed to have *The Truth Commissioner* and to have a novelist of the stature of David Park.

What am I saying, "Northern Ireland is": the entire reading public is fortunate to have it, have him.

Around the time I was starting to write I made a very rash and probably drunken promise to myself that I would have my name on the front of a Booker-worthy novel before I was forty-five. I missed out by a year, but there it is, way down there.

Please welcome the writer whose name is at the top of the jacket, David Park.

This introduction was delivered at the launch of The Truth Commissioner *(Bloomsbury, 2008) at the Linen Hall Library on 12 February, 2008.*

Glenn Patterson was born in 1961 in Belfast and studied on the Creative Writing MA at the University of East Anglia with Malcolm Bradbury. He is the author of six novels, most recently The Third Party *(Blackstaff Press, 2007), as well as a collection of literary journalism,* Lapsed Protestant *(New Island, 2006). He is a Lecturer in Creative Writing at Queen's University Belfast.*

THE ORCHID MAN

Raymond Piper

4 April 1923 – 13 July 2007

Raymond Piper was not a believer (nor indeed am I). Nevertheless, I'll begin with a few beautiful devout lines from the eighteenth-century poet Christopher Smart's *Jubilate Agno*:

> For the flowers are great blessings.
> For the Lord made a nosegay in the meadow with his disciples and
> preached upon the lily.
> For flowers have great virtues for all the senses.
> For the flower glorifies God.
> For the flowers have their angels – even the words of God's
> Creation.
> For the warp and woof of flowers are worked by perpetual moving
> spirits.
> For flowers are good both for the living and the dead.
> For there is a language of flowers.
> For elegant phrases are nothing but flowers.
> For flowers are peculiarly the poetry of Christ.

I drove yesterday from a remote townland in County Mayo, Carrigskeewaun, to celebrate this afternoon the life of my very dear friend Raymond Piper. Several years ago I brought Raymond to Carrigskeewaun and showed him a hummock in front of the cottage. *Spiranthes spirales*, autumn lady's tresses, the loveliest tiny orchid, occasionally grows there – but not, alas, when we visited. Raymond rescued from a sheep-divot a tiny rusty fuse, the ghost of a *spiranthes spirales*, and brought it back to the security of his greenhouse in Belfast. There he cherished it year in, year out.

At our last meeting, about ten days ago, we talked about that hummock and the beautiful plant, the spiral of flowers, ivory-white, I suggested. There was a long silence: "Did you say ivory white? Oh, it is much more subtle than that." He said there was a good chance it would bloom this year. We needed to move it in its pot from the windowsill onto the ground where it would get more moisture. I reminded Raymond of some of our many botanical adventures, mainly in County Clare where he introduced me to the bluest of blues, the blue of spring gentians, and to mountain avens and bloody cranesbill and the beauty of the rare red helleborine swaying against the rocks on Black Head. We spent most of one day looking for bee orchids and fly orchids and found only one fly orchid. But we were rewarded by a cloud of orange-tipped butterflies. And later when we stopped at the ruined church at Kilnaboy to look up at the rude Sheila-na-gig above the door, there at our feet on the rough lawn, completely unanticipated, were dozens of bee orchids.

Most people in Belfast knew Raymond was an artist, and some even referred to him as "the orchid man". Knowing him was the most vivid of experiences – commotion, oddball comedy, a hurly-burly of ideas and information. He was energetic, effervescent, funny, eager – and dapper always: I can picture now the dickey bow and the neat tweeds. Before he went into the hospice he insisted that I take him to the barber's for a last beard and hair trim.

Portraiture was Raymond's main source of income. He is justly celebrated for his portraits of Ulster's grandees and personalities whose features he skilfully captured on canvas. If you go to the Great Hall at Queens or walk down the corridors of the City Hall, you will see his magician's ability to capture a likeness, the inner self as well as the outer, – to convey the complexities of human personality with a few brush strokes or crayon-marks.

But his genius, I feel, found its fullest expression in his botanical studies. Painstaking and passionate, documentary and at the same time visionary, his exquisite "flower portraits" open the doors of perception for both the artist and the scientist in each of us, relating the one to the other at some primordial level.

Raymond illustrated a number of books about Ireland with lovely loose-wristed topographical and architectural drawings. While working on one of these in 1960, he became fascinated with Ireland's wild orchids. Interest grew into obsession and for the next four decades he drove many thousands of miles all over Ireland to study and draw the various species. This turned out to be his life's work.

It is extraordinary that in the age of photography the precision of Raymond's flower paintings should generate such power. "An artist can see things more clearly than a botanist", he explained. But he was both. His paintings are important scientific and historical records as well as works of art. It must have been painful as well as exhilarating for this artist to see the world with such preternatural clarity. In the words of our mutual friend Michael Viney: "Quartering the Burren, the sand dunes of Donegal, the heathland of Fermanagh, his paintings are maps of his life".

At the heart of Raymond Piper's legacy are some two hundred sheets of water-colour paper, several for each of Ireland's thirty or so orchid species. He was planning a book in which the paintings would be reproduced alongside his own scientific commentary. Although it is too late for that now, facsimile publication of the key studies remains an exciting possibility. Another way to honour the hugeness of Raymond's achievement would be to keep his magical flower paintings together in one accessible collection for the enlightenment of future generations. So, waken up, Ulster! Waken up, Ireland! Waken up, the Ulster Museum!

If Raymond had lived in Japan, the government there would long ago have designated him a national treasure. At this precarious time in our planet's history who on this island has produced more relevant work? On his long pilgrimage he took in the entire flora of Ireland – especially, of course, the orchids. I picture him in all weathers, on his hands and knees as though at prayer, paying devout attention to a *neotinea maculata*, an early purple, a fly or a bee orchid, or a marsh heleborine. Let us gratefully salute the sheer magnitude of his solitary enterprise.

More than a decade ago Raymond took me to the Saltee Islands off the South East coast of Ireland. We were looking for insular hybrids. We had hired a small fishing smack. Its name still sounds exactly right to me: Mystical Rose. At our last meeting we talked about one of his most recent studies, this time of a tropical flower, the Cloud Orchid, an exquisite minuscule orchid that grows high up in the misty canopy of the rain forest. Today it is almost too tempting to lay on Raymond Piper's coffin an imaginary Cloud Orchid.

This eulogy was delivered by Michael Longley at Roselawn Crematorium, Belfast, on 18 July 2007.